CRETE

BY
CHRISTOPHER CATLING

Produced by
Thomas Cook Publishing

Written by Christopher Catling
Updated by Mike Gerrard
Original photography by Philip Enticknap and
Ken Paterson
Original design by Laburnum Technologies Pvt Ltd

Editing and page layout by Cambridge Publishing
Management Ltd, Unit 2, Burr Elm Court,
Caldecote CB3 7NU
Series Editor: Karen Beaulah

Published by Thomas Cook Publishing
A division of Thomas Cook Tour Operations Ltd
Company Registration No. 1450464 England

PO Box 227, The Thomas Cook Business Park, Unit 18, Coningsby Road,
Peterborough PE3 8SB, United Kingdom
E-mail: books@thomascook.com
www.thomascookpublishing.com
Tel: +44 (0)1733 416477

ISBN-13: 978-1-84157-689-3

Contents

background   4–19

Introduction   4
The land   6
History   8
Governance   12
Culture   14
Festivals   18

first steps   20–23

what to see   24–145

getting away   146–51

directory   152–88

Shopping   152
Entertainment   158
Children   160
Sport and leisure   162
Food and drink   166
Hotels and accommodation   174
On business   176
Practical guide   178

index   189–91

KEY TO MAPS

✈   Airport

2456m ▲   Mountain

☆   Start of walk/tour

ⓘ   Information

✝   Church

Maps

Crete   4–5
Locator map   5
Eastern Crete   24–5
Iraklíon   28–9
Festós site plan   45
Knossós site plan   54–5
The Lassíthiou plateau tour   88
Cretan archaeology tour   90
Western Crete   94–5
Chaniá   98–9
Réthymno   123
The Thériso Gorge tour   136
The Elafonísi islands tour   138
The Amári Valley tour   140
The Kourtaliotiko Ravine tour   142
The Ímvros Gorge tour   144

Features

Cretan myths   34
Arthur Evans   60
Byzantine churches   84
The Battle of Crete   112
Priests and monks   118
The Cretan menu   164

Walks and tours

Walk: Iraklíon   86
Tour: the Lassíthiou plateau   88
Tour: Cretan archaeology   90
Walk: Chaniá   132
Walk: Réthymno   134
Tour: the Thériso Gorge   136
Tour: the Elafonísi islands   138
Tour: the Amári Valley   140
Tour: the Kourtaliotiko Ravine   142
Tour: the Ímvros Gorge   144

Introduction

Beauty, fertility and the ever-present sea – the aspects of Crete that Homer singled out for mention in the 8th century BC – are still the principal reasons why people come to Crete today. The sea gently laps the golden sands that stretch endlessly along the island's northern shores. The southern coast, by contrast, is broken into a series of smaller coves, many of them remote from any road, but perfect for creating your own private slice of paradise – as many German hippies did in the 1970s.

Byzantine churches are a major feature of the Cretan landscape

Crete's beauty and fertility are features that strike even the most botanically ignorant of visitors if they happen to arrive in spring when the fields, orchards and wayside verges turn into carpets of vividly coloured flowers. That same fertility was the source of the wealth that gave rise to the great Minoan civilisation, which dominated the Aegean from about 2600 BC until some mysterious calamity caused its destruction around 1450 BC.

Crete (Kríti)

Today, the Minoan palace complex at Knossós, just outside Iraklíon, is the island's biggest tourist attraction, though it is just one of hundreds of sites scattered across the island – a legacy of Minoan, Roman, Venetian and Turkish rule. In addition to this, there are some 600 churches and monasteries, many of them decorated with fragments of ancient frescoes, underlining the island's Byzantine heritage.

Exploring Crete

Many visitors come to Crete for its beaches and end up hooked on the island's culture, enjoying the adventure of tracking down a Minoan hilltop sanctuary, or its Christian equivalent, a tiny 12th-century church full of serene icons and wall paintings. Such explorations will take you deeper and deeper into the Cretan countryside, where the majesty of the mountain landscapes and the rhythms of the ordinary life of Crete will undoubtedly work their magic.

Nowhere is that magic more in evidence than in the simple cafés and tavernas of Crete. Choose one in a quiet fishing village and watch the sun go down as you savour the simple local food and wine while listening to the gentle wash of the waves, accompanied by the song of the cicadas. As you relax in the balmy warmth of the evening air, a waiter will appear at your elbow with a dish of fruit or a glass of homemade *raki*, a simple gift from the taverna owner who may later wander over and chat in broken English about his hopes for his grandchildren or his memories of the past. The instinctive warmth of the Cretan character adds another dimension to travel on this richly varied and rewarding island, known appropriately enough to the rest of Greece as *Megalonissos* – the Big Island.

The land

Crete is the largest of the hundreds of islands making up the Grecian archipelago, ranking fifth in the Mediterranean (just behind Sicily, Sardinia, Cyprus and Corsica). The island measures 250km (155 miles) from east to west, but from north to south it is only 60km (37 miles) at its widest and a mere 14km (9 miles) in places. Crete is also the southernmost point of any significance in Europe (only Gávdos – *see p121* – is further south). From Crete to the northern coast of Africa it is only 300km (186 miles) across the Sea of Libya, and Crete lies nearer to the equator than both Tunis and Algiers.

Mountain ranges, once wooded, form the island's central spine

Mountains and caves

Distances on Crete are greatly magnified by the mountain ranges that run like a spine down the centre of the island, acting as a barrier to north-south travel. The southern part of the island has always been more remote and less populated than the north, though this is changing as the little fishing villages of the south are discovered by tourists looking for a quiet base.

Crete's mountains are a continuation of the same chain that sweeps down from the Peloponnese, surfacing again on the islands of Karpathos and Rhodes. They are composed principally of limestone that has been eroded into the spectacular gorges and caves.

It was in one of these caves (the Díktaean – *see p72*) that Zeus, destined to rule over the ancient gods, was born. The story of Zeus is perhaps a mythic throwback to the origin of human life on Crete, since many of the island's caves have revealed extensive evidence of neolithic occupation.

Vegetation

The name of the Ídaean Cave (*see p102*) preserves another memory of the old Crete: *idha* means forest in Doric Greek, and Herodotus, the 5th-century BC Greek historian, refers to Crete as being covered in trees. The island was still well-wooded when the Venetians arrived in the 13th century, but their voracious appetite for ship-building timber, combined with an extensive building programme, began the steady erosion of the indigenous vegetation. Today, only small patches of the original forest survive, consisting of cypress, Calabrian pine and evergreen holm oak, with plane, sweet chestnut and introduced eucalyptus in the river valleys. Taking their cue from the island's ancient forest mix, road builders have planted many new trees to create attractive groves along the verges of the national highway.

The Phrygana

Those areas of Crete that are not under cultivation are covered in a scrub called the *phrygana*, the Cretan equivalent to the *maquis* that covers many parts of the Mediterranean. This fragrant mass of wild plants includes many shrubs that are resistant to the island's sheep and goats. Prickly kermes oak and bitter-tasting euphorbias cover the hillsides in dense billowing mounds of green, with other plants sheltering in and amongst them to take advantage of their protection. These include herbs such as oregano, sage and thyme, shrubs such as phlomis and cistus, and the wonderful range of wildflowers, bulbs and orchids for which Crete is renowned.

Wildlife

The *phrygana* was once home to the splendidly horned Cretan ibex, or *krí-krí*, depicted in Minoan art (see, for example, the Peak Sanctuary Rhyton in Iraklion's Archaeological Museum, *p32*). Walkers on Crete frequently claim to have seen this shy and elusive animal, but they are now virtually extinct on Crete, surviving only in special offshore nature reserves, such as Ayíi Pántes (*see p76*). You are quite likely to spot harmless basking snakes, geckos and wall lizards, and even the occasional chameleon, for though this reptile is a master of camouflage, it gives its presence away by running noisily through the undergrowth. Polecats are common, but most likely to be seen as a roadside accident victim than as a live animal, while the sky is rarely empty of wheeling eagles and vultures searching for young rabbits and other prey.

Typical Cretan scrub, full of tough but fragrant flowering plants

History

6000 BC	Earliest known villages on Crete; neolithic pottery and figurines.
Around 3000 BC	Migrants to Crete establish the first Minoan settlements. The beginning of the pre-Palatial period.
2200 BC	First peak sanctuaries and use of hieroglyphic script.
2000 BC	Beginning of the Old Palace period; trade links with Egypt and the Aegean islands.
1700 BC	Beginning of the New Palace period.
1650 BC	First use of Linear A script.
1550 BC	Artistic peak of Minoan pottery and fresco.
1450 BC	Beginning of the post-Palatial period during which Minoan culture lingered in isolated areas for another 400 years.
1400 BC	Mycenaeans (also known as Achaians) take over the island. Creation of the Linear B script.
1380 BC	Eruption of the volcano on Théra (Santoríni) to which archaeologists of the 19th century attributed the end of Minoan civilisation.
1050 BC	Dorian Greeks arrive in Crete.
650 BC	Extensive trade with Egypt is reflected in the Egyptian influence on Dorian-period art.
450 BC	The Law Code of Gortýs is carved in stone.
69–67 BC	Quintus Metellus invades Crete and ruthlessly destroys many towns and villages. The city of Gortýs becomes the new capital of Roman Crete.
AD 50	St Paul visits Crete and sends St Titus to convert the island's inhabitants to Christianity.
395	Crete comes under eastern Byzantine control and the island's first churches are established.
824	Crete is invaded by the Arabs who use Al-Khandak (Iraklíon) as a base for piratical attacks.
961	The Byzantine general Nikiforos Fokas liberates

	Crete from the Arabs. Byzantine culture begins.		with Greece. Rebellion against the Turks, and harsh reprisals, continue for another 50 years.
1204	Crete is given to one of the Fourth Crusade leaders, Boniface of Montferrat, as his share in the spoils of the war, and he sells the island to Venice.	**1898**	Britain, France, Russia and Italy occupy Crete and force the Ottoman Turks to recognise Crete's right to autonomy.
1263	As a punishment for revolts against Venetian rule, the villages of the Lassíthi plateau are forcibly depopulated and nobody is allowed to farm the area for 200 years.	**1900**	Arthur Evans begins excavating Knossós.
		1913	The Turks are forced to surrender sovereignty over Crete and full union with Greece is achieved.
1453	Constantinople falls to the Turks and Byzantine scholars seek refuge in Crete.	**1941**	Cretans mount heroic resistance against the occupying German forces and suffer appalling reprisals as a result.
1645	The Turks begin their long assault on Crete, taking Chaniá and Réthymno.	**1945**	The Liberation of Crete. Reconstruction of the Cretan economy gets under way.
1669	Crete finally falls to the Turks. Under Turkish rule, rebellion becomes a way of life, leading to tribal opposition from remote mountain strongholds.	**1983**	Mass tourism arrives on Crete, with visitor numbers exceeding 1 million (double the Cretan population) for the first time.
1841	The first of a series of revolts in Crete in support of Enosis – union	**2004/5**	Tourism dips during the Olympic Games but recovers the following year.

The Minoans

Crete is the birthplace of Europe's oldest civilisation, though no-one suspected this until the late 19th century when foreigners were first given permission to conduct limited excavations on the island. Early archaeologists were astounded to discover, not the classical Greek sites they had been expecting, but the accomplished art and architecture of a far older civilisation, comparable in achievement with the other great ancient civilisations of China, Egypt and Mesopotamia.

Ruins of the Palace of Mália

Priests, kings and matriarchs

Arthur Evans (*see pp60–61*) called this culture Minoan after Minos, the legendary king of Crete. Scholars now believe that Minos was not the name of one man, but the title given to all rulers, like the Egyptian term Pharaoh. Minoan rulers were also priests, and their palaces (at Knossós, Málía, Festós and Zákros) were centres for elaborate rituals, in which acrobatic bull-leaping had an important part to play.

This was just one feature of their many-faceted religion: women clearly played an important role, and two of the commonest finds from Minoan temples and peak sanctuaries are clay figures of the bare-breasted Snake Goddess and figures of male devotees with erect penises or large codpieces. Olive trees, which frequently figure in Minoan frescoes and on seals, were also worshipped. All this lends weight to the theory that Minoan religion was rooted in the cycle of the seasons, and that the palaces were centres of annual fertility rituals designed to ensure the success of the crops, probably involving bulls as sacrificial animals.

Old and new palaces

In Minoan chronology, the Old Palace period, from 2000 to 1700 BC, saw the development of massive palaces built around a courtyard, surrounded by clusters of smaller houses and workshops. In 1700 BC an earthquake brought these elaborate palaces tumbling down. During the New Palace period, from 1700 to 1400 BC, the palaces were rebuilt, on the same site, but more elaborate than before, with delicate frescoes and fine furnishings.

Resources and revolution

Minoan society was highly organised, and the power of the priests was based on their control of precious commodities, such as olive oil and wine. Oil was kept in vast quantities in huge jars (*píthoi*) in palace storerooms. Seal stones were used to mark the ownership of these jars, and clay tablets were used for making inventories and keeping accounts. The presence of such a large quantity of inflammable oil contributed greatly to the final destruction of the Minoan civilisation in 1450 BC when fire swept through the palaces.

The evidence of the fires is plain for everyone to see when they visit Minoan palace sites, but the precise cause is shrouded in speculation and mystery. Evans confidently blamed the eruption of Théra (Santoríni), but that took place in 1380 BC. Other historians have put forward the theory that Crete was invaded and sacked, perhaps by the Mycenaeans who later came to control Crete, but there is no archaeological evidence to support this.

Post-palatial period

In the post-palatial period, from 1400 to 1100 BC, the Mycenaeans took advantage of the disaster that befell Crete and moved in, briefly occupying the palace at Knossós and using it as the administrative centre of the island until 1200 BC when the palace was finally abandoned. Some peak sanctuaries continued in use, and there are echoes of the Minoan golden age in the Mycenaean-influenced sculpture and pottery of this era.

Some Cretans clung on to the old ways for generations; they are mentioned in Homer's *Odyssey* (written down around 700 BC) where, when mentioning the Minoans and Mycenaeans who live on Crete, he mentions the 'Etocretans (ie the true, or genuine, Cretans), proud of their native stock'. Right up until the 3rd century BC they maintained their own separate language and script, dubbed Linear B, which is seen on inscriptions that have been found at Praisós and Dréros. It intrigued archaeologists for a long time until it was finally deciphered by Professor John Chadwick and architect Mark Ventris in 1952.

The west façade and grand staircase of the palace at Festós

Governance

Cretans are a fiercely proud and independent-minded people who, in the words of a popular phrase, see themselves as 'Cretans first, Greeks second'. They are also fond of naming their children Eleftherias (Freedom) and of quoting the patriotic slogan, 'Freedom or Death' that anti-Turkish rebels adopted as their battle cry in the 19th century (Kazantzákis later used it as the title for one of his novels). In reality, Cretans have experienced little in the way of true political freedom over the last 3,500 years.

The flag of Greece

A history of oppression
Since the collapse of the Minoan civilisation, the island has been ruled by one foreign power after another – Mycenaeans, Dorian Greeks, Romans, Arabs, Byzantines, Venetians, Turks and Egyptians.

Plateía Eleftherías (Freedom Square), Iraklíon

The 20th century brought long-awaited unification with the rest of Greece, and the Cretan statesman, Eleftherias Venizélos, served as prime minister of Greece on numerous occasions, playing a central role in national politics and foreign affairs between 1896 and 1935.

Following World War II and invasion by Germany (*see p112*), Crete came under the Greek Colonels' dictatorship from 1967 until 1974. That year, following a popular referendum, Greece abolished the monarchy and, along with Crete, become a parliamentary democracy, headed by a president.

National government
Even now, Crete has little political autonomy, for Greece has a strongly centralised government, with a parliament in Athens. Crete sends elected representatives, called deputies, to the parliament, and one Cretan politician, Kostas Mitsotakis, rose to lead the right-of-centre ND (Néa Dhimokratía, or New Democracy) party which narrowly won

The PASOK party's sunrise symbol

the 1990 election. The other dominant political force is PASOK (The Pan Hellenic Socialist Movement). Its founder, Andreas Papandreou, was succeeded in 1996 by Costas Simitis, who modernised the party and was successful in two general elections. Despite his record, however, PASOK was voted out in 2004 and the ND party took control once more.

Local government

Crete has no independent regional government, and is ruled instead by governors appointed by the ruling party in Athens. There is one governor for each of the island's four provinces (*nomoi*), namely Chaniá, Réthymno, Iraklíon and Lassíthiou. In the past, Cretan governors and political leaders have modelled themselves on the clan leaders of old, whose proud portraits look down from the walls of the history museums in Chaniá and Iraklíon. Refusing to be 'yes men', they have frequently defied the national party line in the greater interests of Crete. That is changing, however, and the availability of new development funds from the European Union means that their energies are focused on securing the maximum benefit for the island.

Crete as a military base

Though the presence of large numbers of NATO military personnel and weaponry is hotly debated, Cretans are only too well aware that they stand between the Islamic world and the West, and are therefore a potential target in the event of aggression. The one thing that prevents them from demanding an end to the NATO presence is the thought that Turkey might offer it a new home, thus gaining valuable military and economic aid at Crete's expense.

Farming the old way

Culture

On Crete two separate cultures co-exist side by side: the Crete of the 21st century and the rural, pre-industrial Crete, which has not changed much, in any essential respect, since Minoan times.

Country life

In the heart of rural Crete there are still many people, mainly elderly now, who live a very meagre, self-sufficient life. Their food comes from what they grow, or gather wild. Though every village now has electricity, homes are simple and cooking is still done over a wood fire. They rarely travel far beyond their home village, and when they do, they go by donkey, which also serves as an all-purpose pack animal.

These people are the survivors of the old Cretan way of life. Their children have left this (and them) behind, seeking paid work and an air-conditioned apartment in one of Crete's burgeoning towns, or emigrating to work on a building site or in a Greek restaurant far from home. The remaining rural Cretans claim to have an egalitarian society, without class distinctions or rancour, and the warm-heartedness of their easy-going hospitality appears to bear this out. They attribute their way of life to centuries of subjugation to foreign rulers, especially the harsh and oppressive Turks. Taxed into abject poverty and denied education or legal rights, they developed their own unwritten codes of honour, mutual respect and co-operation that have survived to this day.

The Kafeníon

Within this society, the *kafeníon*, or café, also serves the purpose of local parliament. The typical village *kafeníon* is as plain as can be: no posters adorn the walls and there are no price lists or tempting bottles of exotic drinks on display. Local wine, coffee and water are the principal drinks on offer: customers can linger for hours over one small drink and nobody will object. On the contrary, it would be thought odd not to linger, since the *kafeníon* is the local club, a place where men can gather to spend the whole evening in talk or play a game of backgammon. Cafés are traditionally male-dominated establishments.

The Voltá

Women have their equivalent in the *voltá*, the evening stroll, a habit influenced by the Italian *passeggiata*, introduced by the Venetians. The *voltá* takes place at that delightful hour of the day when darkness begins to fall and work is done. As the sun sets and the swifts flit above the tree tops, women take off their aprons, brush their hair and step out of doors. Taking their children they stroll arm in arm to greet old friends, to gossip or, if they are still young and single, to flirt.

Country v. town

The *voltá* and the *kafenío* are the two traditions that still link the old Crete with the new. The evening stroll in Réthymno is especially vibrant, and the large number of students in both Chaniá and Réthymno help to ensure that the cafés used by local people are always full – especially late at night, long after hard-working rural Cretans have gone to bed. Country rarely meets town except for village festivities, weddings, baptisms and funerals, or on the one day a week (often a Saturday) when rural Cretans descend on their nearest big town to set up street stalls selling everything from honey, olives and dried herbs, to leather boots and hand-knitted sweaters. Arriving the night before market day, many give up the attempt to snatch some sleep in the back of their van or pick-up truck, drifting to the local cafés where the music and dancing go on until the first light of dawn.

Customs and etiquette

Cretan people are very friendly, if a little shy, on meeting strangers. A wave or a nod as you pass someone while out walking usually elicits a broad smile. If you say hello in Greek, all the better. Don't be surprised to be offered a piece of fruit off somebody's orange tree or a glass of *raki* on the house in a restaurant – or even a little extra dish you did not order. Such spontaneous generosity is still quite common, especially in the parts of Crete not tainted by mass tourism. Cretans love to practise their English, so take the time to chat – about the weather, children, your job – all are subjects with endless potential.

Both club and parliament, the *kafenion* is a male-dominated institution

Tapestry depicting a well-dressed Cretan couple

Costume

Cretan costume is still worn with pride by some country Cretans, especially by the older men who gather to pass the day playing backgammon in the *kafenion*. Prior to the Turkish occupation of Crete, dress consisted of a simple belted tunic for both men and women. Examples can be seen in many church frescoes throughout the island. Typically, the donor of the fresco (and his wife) is depicted beside the door of the church, and these portraits show that costume changed little in the period from the 11th to the 16th century (copies of these are displayed in Iraklíon's Historical Museum – *see p36*).

Turkish fashions

The Turks introduced baggy breeches (called *vraka*) which Cretans adopted in a major break with their past. Ironically it was the anti-Turkish rebels who were keenest on this new fashion (today, Cretan men are more likely to wear ordinary riding breeches). Waistcoats are worn over a simple shirt by men and women alike, usually embroidered with colourful motifs that differ from region to region. Women also wear skirts of brightly coloured stripes, protected by a simple apron. Men adopted the black crochet-work cap with its distinctive fringe as a symbol of mourning for their island under Turkish occupation, though the cap continues to be worn to this day.

Daggers and boots

On special occasions (such as weddings and feast days), men still wear a big silk sash around their waist, into which they tuck a whole collection of heirlooms – perhaps a tobacco horn, perhaps a silver dagger or a pistol (often an antique 18th-century weapon, last used in World War II). Smart and highly polished riding boots complete the picture, along with a moustache. Fine examples of historic costume are displayed in the Historical Museums at Iraklíon (*see p36*), Chaniá (*see p97*), and at the Museum of Cretan Ethnology in Vóroí (*see p78*).

The Cretan shepherd

Drive along any rural road in Crete and it will not be long before you encounter a flock of sheep or goats with an attendant shepherd, probably seated nearby beneath the shade of an olive tree. Stop on any rural road and you will hear the musical clamour of bells. Traditionally, long bells are hung round the necks of goats and wide ones round sheep, with seven different sizes and notes so that the shepherd can identify each individual in his flock. The shepherd who spends his lifetime looking after these hardy foragers will probably be dressed in a fine pair of knee boots, baggy Cretan pantaloons, and lace headcap if he is over 40 years of age, and nearby will be a donkey carrying a wooden pack saddle and panniers.

Times are changing, however, and younger shepherds are more likely to be dressed in jeans and trainers and driving a pick-up truck. Regardless of age, all shepherds carry a crook, whose shape varies from region to region. Shepherding is a hard and lonely life, and although both lamb and *feta* cheese are staples of the Cretan diet, it is rare to find a wealthy farmer – one reason why fewer and fewer young people take up shepherding, aspiring instead to a more comfortable office job.

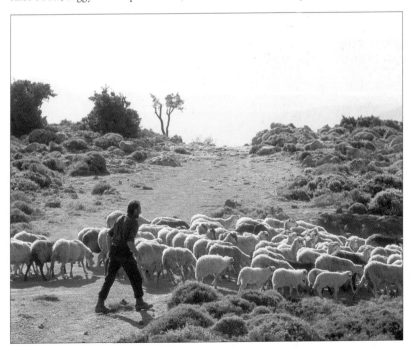

The lonely figure of a shepherd searching for green pastures

Festivals

Easter is the big festival on Crete and many people come to the island just for this seven-day period of religious and secular spectacle. Bear in mind, though, that the dates of Easter and most other religious festivals vary from year to year, and do not always coincide with those of the calendar of the Western church.

A traditional Easter breakfast of red-dyed eggs

Easter rites

Good Friday (Epitafiós) is marked by solemn processions in which a shrouded bier, representing the dead Christ, is carried around the village to the accompaniment of prayers and mournful song. At midnight the following day, Easter Saturday, all lights are extinguished and the priest produces the first flame of the new Christian year, symbolising resurrection and renewal. Holy Light, as this is called, is brought from Jerusalem where the first holy candle is lit. Members of the congregation light their candles from this flame to the chant of *Khristós anésti*

Traditional dance plays an important role in Cretan life

(Christ is Risen). This marks the end of the service, when church bells peal, firecrackers explode and, in some districts, bonfires are lit on which a dummy, representing Judas, the disciple who betrayed Christ, is burnt. Easter Sunday is then spent in feasting, traditionally on spit-roasted lamb.

Saints' days

Lamb features again on the Feast of Ágios Giórgios (St George, celebrated on 23 April, or, if Orthodox Easter happens to be very late in the month, on the Monday and Tuesday after Easter Sunday). St George is very popular on Crete because, amongst his many other responsibilities, he is the patron of shepherds. Sheep and goat farmers take their flocks to church to be blessed, and one of their number is sacrificed to provide the traditional St George's Day dish of charcoal-grilled, herb-and-rice-stuffed lamb.

Every Cretan village also celebrates its own saint's day with a church service followed by singing, dancing, drinking and feasting. Visitors are warmly welcomed, so ask at the tourist office for details of any village name days coming up in the vicinity at the time of your visit. One that is certain to be celebrated all over the island, given that many churches are dedicated to the Panagia (the Virgin Mary), is 15 August, the Feast of the Assumption.

Wine and food

Amongst the most appealing festivals for atmosphere are those held in different parts of the island from early August to the end of October, an excuse for

Candle flames for the Resurrection

finishing off last year's wine and sampling this year's *raki*. More of an acquired taste is Kholidovradia (The Night of the Snails), celebrated by the mollusc-loving inhabitants of Vámos in April. Autumn brings the chestnut harvest in Élos, and with it an excuse to eat chestnut-flavoured sweets of all kinds, washed down with yet more *raki*, on the first Sunday after 20 October.

Arts festivals

Throughout the main holiday month of August, major towns mount one- or two-week arts festivals; a feast of dancing, parades, music, theatre, and exhibitions of paintings and crafts.

Impressions

The idea of touring Crete by car and stopping somewhere different every night has yet to catch on. The lack of direct scheduled flights to Crete and the scarcity of charter flight-only deals means most tourists have to travel on a package, booking accommodation in advance. Island wandering is recommended during the quieter times of year when more flight-only deals are available, hotels have rooms to spare and temperatures are ideal for walking.

Scooters and cars can be hired in nearly every town or resort

Crete's tourist season only lasts from Easter to October. However, the island is currently embarking on a winter pilot programme to encourage year-round tourism, and more upmarket resorts and boutique hotels have been built.

East or west, north or south?
An alternative to going wherever you please is to choose one hotel or villa that is centrally located for the area you want to explore. This means basing yourself in the north of the island where the national highway provides a relatively swift route from east to west. Even so, Crete is far too large to see in one week, or even in a fortnight. The best you can hope to do in two weeks is to explore the eastern or the western half of the island, choosing your base accordingly.

The east of Crete is best for those who want to see the main archaeological sites. To explore this region, you could do worse than choose a base on the coastal strip between Iraklíon and Ágios Nikólaos. Here you will be within easy reach of the palaces at Knossós, Mália,

Festós and Zákros, and within easy driving distance of the Lassíthiou plateau and Díktaean Cave (Dhiktaio Andro). Be warned, though, that this is the most developed part of Crete, so you have to choose your base carefully, paying more, perhaps, for a villa in a village rather than ending up in a cheap but anonymous apartment in one of the tourist ghettos, such as Mália and Chersonísou.

Hiking and flowers
The further west you go on Crete, the quieter it gets, although there is another flurry of tourist development around Chaniá. Western Crete is generally greener, more mountainous and less intensively farmed than the plains that make up so much of eastern Crete. Nature lovers will find that the west is far richer, botanically, and for historically inclined visitors, there is a greater concentration of Byzantine churches to explore. Above all, this is the region for long and spectacular walks through the Samaria and Ínvros gorges (Farángi Samariás and Farángi Ínvros),

or out along the finger-like peninsulas of the northern coast.

Beach holidays

If you just want to drop out and do nothing more energetic than strolling to the beach each day, there are scores of semi-tropical hideaways in the less developed extremities of the island, from Vái, in the extreme east of the island, to the Elafonísi islands in the extreme west. Most are on the south side of the island, with characterful fishing villages such as Palaióchora, Chóra Sfakíon and Mátala, known for their unspoilt Cretan character, good shops, food and nightlife. Accommodation availability in these villages is very limited, so book early in the season, using tour operators who specialise in the lesser known parts of the island.

Getting around

If you know you want to do a lot of touring on Crete, it is cheaper to pre-book a hire car as part of your holiday package. However, if you decide to wait until you arrive in Crete, you will find scores of car rental agents on the main street of every Cretan town.

It is vital to check the state of the tyres (including the spare) before setting out on any journey, and be sure that you know how to use the jack – potholes and sharp stones make punctures on Crete's rural roads common. Motorbikes and scooters are also readily available for hire, but are not suitable for long journeys. Despite the fact that many Cretans break the law, wearing a helmet is compulsory – ensure that the hire company gives you one that fits you comfortably and is not damaged.

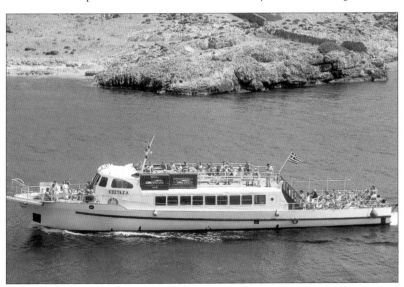

Cruising to Eloúnta is a good way to see the picturesque coast

Rural churches may be difficult to reach but are usually open all the time

A serene pastoral vista of rural Crete

Museums and archaeological sites

Cretans are early risers, making the most of the coolest part of the day and taking a long siesta during the afternoon. Opening times reflect this, with many museums and sites open for the morning and early afternoon only (typically 8.30am–3pm).

Photography is no longer permitted in museums and on sites. However, professional photographers may apply for special permission from the Ministry of Culture. At Knossós (where the site guards are unusually truculent, and prone to go on strike regularly to protest about their grievances) it is possible that you may not even be allowed to carry a camera on to the site without paying the extra fee.

Officially, it is forbidden to climb on the walls at archaeological sites, but this rule is widely ignored. You will also find that sites are, quite literally, littered with pieces of ancient pottery. Do not give in to temptation – picking them up is also against the law, as is any kind of unlicensed digging.

Monasteries and churches

Monasteries are generally open to visitors from 8am to 1pm or 2pm, though some reopen at 3pm or 5pm until 7pm. All insist on modest dress (shorts, sleeveless shirts and beachwear are forbidden in many) so it is sensible to carry a change of clothes if you go visiting a monastery.

The opening arrangements for churches vary considerably. Some are open all the time, but many are kept locked. It is common practice to begin the hunt for the key (*kleidí*) at the nearest *kafeníon* (café), but it is not good manners to do so during the 1–5pm siesta hours.

Often the key is held by the local priest (*pappás*) who may accompany you to the church and provide an enthusiastic commentary, in broken English, on the principal frescoes and icons. If so, you will be expected to give the priest a small donation towards church funds. Remember, too, that women are not supposed to enter the sanctuary (the area behind the iconostasis, or screen) unless invited.

A typical Byzantine church at Samonás

Eastern Crete

Eastern Crete is made up of the two provinces (*nomoi*) of Iraklíon and Lassíthiou. This is the most heavily populated part of the island, with 292,000 people living in Iraklíon province (140,000 of them in Iraklíon city alone) and 78,000 in Lassíthiou (19,000 in the capital, Ágios Nikólaos). Together these two provinces account for almost 62 per cent of the total Cretan population of 603,000.

Lake Voulisméni, in Ágios Nikólaos

The resort coast

The city of Iraklíon is the main gateway to the island, with a ferry port and international airport. Around 70 per cent

Eastern Crete

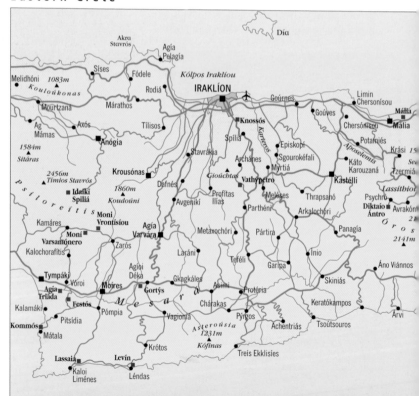

of the 2 million tourists who come to Crete every year stay in one of the resorts strung out along the 70-km (43-mile) coastal strip along the north coast stretching east of Iraklíon, especially the resort towns of Chersonísou, Mália, Eloúnta and Ágios Nikólaos. Staying in any of these places you will not lack for shops, cocktail bars, nightlife or the company of fellow visitors, but you will experience very little of the true Crete.

Beaches

The coastal strip east of Iraklíon is one long series of resorts, many of them offering shops, fast-food outlets, and beach loungers for hire. If you want to escape the crowds, head for the far east of the island, or the less developed beaches on the south coast. Remoteness does not guarantee isolation, however, the so-called Palm Beach at Vaí and the beach at Préveli are among the most crowded on the island at peak season. Bathing nude is strictly forbidden.

An undeserved reputation

Both provincial capitals have suffered at the hands of writers who have exaggerated their less attractive features.

Eastern Crete has some excellent and very popular beaches such as this one at Mália

Iraklíon is often portrayed as the ultimate urban jungle of dusty and noisy streets and bumper-to-bumper horn-blowing traffic. For much of the time Iraklíon is, in fact, a quiet and surprisingly civilised city with a characterful open-air market, much interesting (if dilapidated) architecture, and an archaeological museum whose contents can compete with the best that Greece has to offer.

Ágios Nikólaos has also been ill-served by press and politicians who have dubbed it the 'lager-lout capital of Europe', but this is by no means a town of rabid hooligans on the rampage – rather it is Eastern Crete's most picturesque town, set around a natural lake, with many excellent restaurants and shops.

Iraklíon province

It was here that the Minoan civilisation first arose and where the most spectacular archaeological sites are to be found. Three of the four major Minoan palaces, which formed the focal point for Minoan art and industry, are located here (at Knossós, Mália and Festós), along with smaller palace complexes at Agía Triáda and Archánes. Festós and Agía Triáda enjoy the most spectacular locations on the fertile agricultural plain on Messará.

Lassíthiou

The other important Minoan palace is at Zákros, in Lassíthiou province, at the extreme eastern end of the island. Lassíthiou is a mountainous province, famous as the birthplace of the mighty Zeus. His mother, Rhea, sought out the privacy of the Díktaean Cave for her confinement so that the infant god might not suffer the same fate as his siblings and be eaten by their father, Kronos (*see p34*).

Today, there is little privacy to be had at the cave, which has become one of the major tourist attractions on Crete, featuring on coach excursions along with the windmill-covered Lassíthiou plain, which sits in a bowl, entirely encircled by high peaks, just to the south of Mália.

The south coast

This being Crete, the opportunity to escape from the crowds is never very far away, and true solitude can be experienced on the southern coast, much of which is accessible only by dirt roads and footpaths. Here, adventurous travellers can track down hermits' caves and monasteries clinging to the cliffs.

How long this will continue to be true remains to be seen. Bulldozers have already begun to open up a new south-coast road and concrete villas are spreading rapidly around any tiny village with access to a sandy beach. It seems inevitable that tourism will increase along the southern coast, and in the fairly unspoiled southeastern corner of the island, especially with the increased use of the airport at Sitía. At present, though, development is fairly slow, and tourism numbers reasonably steady rather than booming.

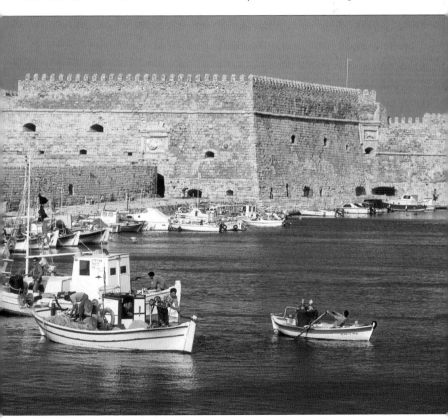

Yachts and fishing boats moor beneath the protective walls of Iraklíon's Venetian Fort

Iraklíon

Iraklíon, capital of Crete, is the fifth-largest city in Greece. The air raids of 1941 reduced the city to rubble so that it lacks the old-world charm of Réthymno or Chaniá. Though no great beauty, Iraklíon can at least claim to be prosperous, with the highest per capita income of any city in Greece, derived from a combination of shipping, banking and tourism. The city's star attraction is the Archaeological Museum (*see p30*), full of Minoan treasures, many excavated at Knossós (*see p52*) just 5km (3 miles) to the south.

The harbour

Iraklíon's historic harbour bustles with luxury yachts and fishing boats unloading their catch beneath the protective walls of the bulky Venetian fort. The first fort was built here in 1303 but this was later destroyed by an earthquake. The fort was rebuilt between 1523 and 1540, and was to play a key role in the Great Siege of 1647–69. At the end of this 22-year siege, one of the longest in history, the Venetians finally gave up one of their most precious possessions, surrendering Iraklíon (and Crete) to the Turks, but only after heroic resistance, in which 30,000 Venetians and 118,000 Turks met their deaths. The new Turkish rulers of Iraklíon changed little, and even the Lion of St Mark, symbol of Venice, still stands guard over the entrance to the fort.

Another legacy of Venetian rule is the 16th-century Arsenal where ships of the Venetian naval fleet were once built, repaired and fitted out for battle. A busy

Iraklíon town plan (see pp86–7 for walk)

Kólpos Iraklíou

Koúles

Palaió
Limáni

ODÓS SOFOKLI

VENIZÉLOU

Ruins of
Ágios Pétros

O THEOTOKOPOULON

Arsenáli

Istorikó
Mouseío
Krítis

Ágios
Dimítrios

25 AVGOUSTOU

Katholikí
Ekklisía

Arsenáli

PLATEÍA
KOUNTORYOTON

ODÓS EPIMENÍDOU

IKARÍOU

ODÓS

ODÓS EPIMENÍDOU

ODÓS MALIKOÚTI

Sabionera
Bastion

Priuli
Fountain

CHANDAKÓS

GIAMALAKI

ODÓS MIRIONOU

Párko
Gkréko

Ágios
Títos

O AG TITOU

ODÓS

PLATEÍA
VENIZÉLOU
Kríni
Morozíni

Loggia

MIRAMPELOU

ODÓS MIRAMPELOU

Archaiologikó
Mouseío

ODÓS BOFOR

ASTRALA

KALOKAIRINOU

O AYMNA

ODÓS

Agía
Aikateríni

Ágios
Minás

PL. N
FOKA

ODÓS IDIS

Ágios
Márcos

ODÓS IDOMÍNEOS

ODÓS DAIDÁLOS

ODÓS DIKAIOSÍNIS

i

NIKOLATOU

ODÓS MONIS KARDIOTISSIS

Ágios Minás
Cathedral

KYRILOU LOUKAREOS

PL AG
AIKATERÍNI

KATECHAKI

ODÓS 1821

Agorá

ODÓS 1866

Touristikí
Astynomía

PLATEÍA
DAKALOGIANI

PLATEÍA
ELEFTHERÍAS

St George's
Gate

ODÓS IKAROU

ODÓS
ANTHEMIOU

ODÓS
ARFIMIDOUS

ODÓS KARTÉROU

Kríni
Bembo

ODÓS AVEROF

L. DIMOKRATÍAS

TOMBAZI

O VIKELA

PLATEÍA
KORNAROU

ODÓS EVANS

ODÓS

ODÓS PINALOGKAS

Panagía
Stavroforou

GAMPOUDI MOUSOUROU

ODÓS PEDIADOS

Public
Gardens

ODÓS NIKOUSIOU

ODÓS EVANS

ODÓS PEDIAKOS

St George's
Bastion

DIMOKRATÍAS

ODÓS GERONIMAKI

Ágios
Andréas

Kondiláki
Gate

ODÓS

PLASTIRA

NIKOLAOU

Jesus
Gate

Jesus
Bastion

PLATEÍA
KIPROU

L. CHARILÁOU TRIKOUPI

GEORGIADOU

ODÓS DRAKONTOPOULOU

ODÓS KASTRINAKI

ODÓS MISSONOS

Táfos
Kazantzáki

Martinengo
Bastion

ODÓS

road has since cut these huge vaulted
buildings off from the harbour, but they
remain an impressive tribute to Venetian
marine engineering.

*Venetian fort open: Apr–Oct,
daily 8.30am–3pm.
Closed: Sun in winter.
Admission charge.*

The ramparts and tomb of Kazantzákis

Contemporary with the Fort and the Arsenal are the walls that enclose Iraklíon for a total length of 3km (2 miles). It is possible to walk the complete circuit for views of city gardens and rooftops, but in order to gain a sense of the massive proportions of the walls it is best to visit Porta Kenoúria, the gate on Odós Evans in the south of the city. Built in 1538 by the great Italian architect, Michele Sanmicheli, the walls stand 18m (59ft) tall and over 40m (131ft) thick. On the Martinengo Bastion, five minutes' walk to the southwest, is the simple grave of the Cretan novelist, Níkos Kazantzákis (*see p68*). He was buried here at his own request, and the inscription on his tomb says much about the Cretan attitude to life and mortality: 'I hope for nothing, I fear nothing, I am free.'

Archaeological Museum

This is rated one of the top museums in Greece because of the quality of the objects on display. The sheer number of visitors can be a problem so allow longer than you would expect to tour the museum, or come during lunch hour when there are far fewer tour groups.

Room I

This room is devoted to the neolithic and pre-palatial phase of Cretan history (6000–2000 BC). Here we see the first depictions of bulls and acrobats, of the female fertility deity with exaggerated hips, breasts and buttocks, of the symbolic double-bladed axe, and of the *moclos* – the sacred double horn emblem. These motifs recur again and again, honed and refined over 3,000 years of production.

Among the assorted exhibits, the highlights are the pottery rattle (between Cases 4 and 5), with a tracing alongside of the scene from the Harvester Vase (*see* Room VII *p32*), showing such a rattle in use; and the wonderfully naturalistic pot lid in Case 7 with a handle shaped like a dog.

Rooms II and III

These two rooms are devoted to the Old Palace period (2000–1700 BC). A delightful insight into the sophistication of

Headless statue outside the Iraklíon Archaeological Museum

IRAKLÍON'S NAME

The bustling capital of Crete started out as a Minoan harbour, named Heraklion (city of Herakles, that is, Hercules) by the Dorian Greeks. In 824, under Saracen rule, it became Rabdh el Khanadak (Castle of the Ditch), was corrupted to Khandakas and later, under Venetian rule, to Candia. This was the name under which the city, and the whole island, was known until the end of Turkish rule in 1898, when the Dorian Greek name was revived, as Iraklíon in modern Greek spelling.

architecture at the time is given by
the so-called Town Mosaic (Case 25),
consisting of a number of pottery
squares painted with representations
of Minoan houses.

There are numerous clay figurines
from peak sanctuaries, pointing to their
heads or stomachs, perhaps indicating
bits of their bodies that they want
curing. Women wear bell-shaped skirts
and place their hands under their
breasts, pushing them up in a gesture of
offering, whilst men have erect penises
or large codpieces.

Room III contains masterpieces of
Minoan pottery, such as the vase with
the daisy motif (Case 36) and the
lifelike clay pig in the last case on the
right. Here too is the famous circular
clay disc from Festós (Case 41), bearing
a stamped inscription that has so far
defeated all attempts at interpretation.

Room IV
This is the first of six rooms devoted to
the New Palace period (1700–1450 BC),
with outstanding works from the palace

at Knossós. One is a gaming board made
of ivory and precious stone (Case 57).
In Case 49 is a lovely vase covered in an
all-over pattern of bamboo leaves. Case
51 contains the famous Bull's Head
Rhyton, a gentle-looking beast carved
out of steatite, with gilded wooden
horns, rock crystal eyes and inlaid shell
nostrils. Sacred libations – perhaps of
bull's blood or wine – were poured from
a hole behind the horns.

Case 56 contains a delicate ivory
figure of an acrobat flying through
the air in mid-manoeuvre, probably
having launched himself from the
horns of a bull. Case 52 is full of stone
vases covered in intricate designs –
see the one entitled 'The Entrapped
Octopus', for example.

Case 50 brings us face to face with
the Snake Goddess, a frightening figure
when viewed close up, with bulging eyes
that seek to entrance the onlooker –
or is it the goddess herself that is in a
trance? Next to her is another similar
figure crawling with snakes that entwine
her hair, dress and belt.

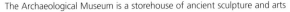
The Archaeological Museum is a storehouse of ancient sculpture and arts

Room V

This room contains material excavated from parts of Knossós away from the main palace, including the workshops and houses lining the Royal Road. An idea of what these houses may have looked like is indicated by the clay model in Case 70a. Pictures on the walls of this room show reconstructions of various parts of Knossós drawn by Piet de Jong, the draughtsman who worked with Sir Arthur Evans during the excavation of the site.

Room VI

Here the most rewarding exhibits are in the central cases, where gold and ivory jewellery is displayed, including necklace ornaments and rings shaped like shells, bulls' heads, lions and ducks.

Room VII

This contains the finest example of Minoan jewellery ever found, an exquisite pendant of gold depicting two bees, joined at the mouth and tail, leaving a drop of honey on a honeycomb held between their legs (Case 101). Equally enthralling are three stone vases. The subject of the Chieftain Cup (Case 95) is still being debated: does it show a hunting party, or a Minoan chieftain being presented with hides as some form of tax or tribute? The Boxer Rhyton (Case 96) shows the now-familiar sport of bull-leaping, as well as scenes of boxing and wrestling. The marvellous Harvester Vase (Case 94) shows a procession of youths carrying rods and pitchforks, accompanied by singers and musicians, taking part in some kind of harvest festival.

Room VIII

The finest of all the Minoan libation vases is the Peak Sanctuary Rhyton (Case 111). Not only is the carving wonderfully naturalistic, with wild tulips blossoming from the craggy heights, Cretan wild goats with magnificent horns resting on the mountain ridges, and crows using the sacred bull's horn symbol on the temple roof as a perch, it also provides a detailed view of the appearance of a Minoan peak sanctuary of the type otherwise known only from excavated ruins.

Also in this room are numerous fine examples of pottery shaped like shells and decorated with marine symbols, and the famous libation vase of black crystal – the finest piece to be found in the Zakaros Palace.

Room IX

The marine motifs continue with an especially enjoyable octopus flask to be found in Case 120.

Rooms X to XIII

Exhibits dating to the post-Minoan era (1400–500 BC) show new developments, and the introduction of Egyptian influences to Minoan art. Though the objects are more primitive, and the decoration more debased, there are some unusual figures, including the Poppy Goddess (Room X, Case 133) and the woman on a swing (Room X, Case 143). The displays on the ground floor end with a roomful of clay sarcophagi, shaped like bathtubs.

Rooms XIV to XVI

Much of the first floor of the museum is devoted to Minoan frescoes, forming the highlight of the collection. The archaeologists who reconstructed these works, often from a tiny handful of fragments, have been accused of using their imaginations too freely, but it is difficult not to be moved by the great vibrancy and naturalism displayed by the Partridge Frieze, or the Leaping Dolphins.

Problems of interpretation are well illustrated by the display in Room XVI where a fresco, previously thought to depict a boy picking flowers (entitled the 'Saffron Gatherer'), has now been reassembled to create a bigger picture called the 'Blue Monkey', set in a landscape of rocks and crocuses.

Completely original is the wonderful stone sarcophagus in the centre of Room XIV, its painted decoration of aquamarine blue and ox-blood red still remarkably fresh. The long sides depict a funeral procession in great detail, showing a horse-drawn chariot, the sacrifice of a young bull, and various musical instruments.

Rooms XVII to XX
The last part of the museum is devoted to Greek and Roman antiquities, which seem almost lifeless compared with the exuberance of the preceding frescoes. An occasional exhibit stands out, such as the life-size statue of a boy in bronze (Room XVIII), found at Ierápetra and dating from the 1st century BC.
Plateía Eleftherias. Tel: (2810) 226092. The museum closed recently for a short period of renovation. Telephone for latest information.

Classical Greek heads and sculptured stone bear testimony to the artisan's skill

The birth of Zeus

The myth begins in the time of the Titans, the primeval sons of Gaia (the Earth) and Uranus (the Heavens). Kronos (Time), the youngest of the Titans, had already dethroned his own father and castrated him in order to become king. Now, he was in the habit of swallowing his own children at birth to prevent them from robbing him of his kingship. Fed up with the loss of five children, Rhea, his wife (and sister), hid deep in the Díktaean Cave on Crete to give birth to Zeus. Kronos got to hear of the birth and demanded his usual meal, but was given a stone wrapped in swaddling clothes instead. Zeus, meanwhile, was hidden in the Idaean Cave where he was protected by the young warrior, Kourites, and the goat, Amalthia, who provided everything for the baby from its horn.

Minos and the Minotaur

In time, Zeus came to overthrow his father and establish his throne on Mount Olympus. One day he fell in love with Europa, the daughter of King Aghinor, ruler of Phinicia. He appeared in the guise of a bull, carried Europa away on his back and impregnated her. Europa gave birth to King Minos, who, with the guidance of his father, Zeus, ruled Crete wisely. His happiness was, however, shattered by Pasiphae, his licentious wife. She too fell in love with a white bull (this time not a god in disguise), and asked Daidalos, artist and inventor, for help. He built her a wooden cow covered in hide. In this disguise, Pasiphae was mounted by the bull. The fruit of this bestial union was the monstrous Minotaur, half-man, half-bull, who terrorised the court of King Minos until Daidalos invented an endless labyrinth, within which the beast was ensnared.

Theseus outwits the Minotaur

The Minotaur had to be fed seven male and seven female virgins every seven years from the city of Athens. This was the penalty the Athenians had to pay for having killed Androgo, son of Minos. One year, Prince Theseus, son of the Athenian king, Aegeus, intending to slay the Minotaur, volunteered to be one of the victims. On Crete, he was assisted by Ariadne, the daughter of King Minos, who gave him a ball of wool. Attaching one end of the wool to the door of the labyrinth, Theseus was able to retrace his steps and escape once he had killed the Minotaur. Theseus then set sail for Athens, taking Ariadne with him, though he

subsequently abandoned her on the island of Naxos. When Theseus arrived back in Athens he forgot to hoist a white sail to signal his safe return. His father, Aegeus, assumed that his son had been killed by the Minotaur and leapt into the sea, which has been called the Aegean ever since in his honour.

Facing page: the infant Zeus
Above: Theseus and Ariadne

The Historical Museum of Crete

The Historical Museum takes up where the Archaeological Museum (*see p30*) leaves off, and follows Crete's chequered history into the 20th century.

Basement

This area displays sculptures and architectural fragments dating back to the Venetian occupation of the island. Doorways and windows, angels, saints, coats of arms, and tombstones bearing Turkish, Armenian and Jewish inscriptions, indicate the cosmopolitan nature of the island's port.

Ground floor

The excellent new AG Kalokairinos room covers the Christian period, with emphasis on Venetian rule and the Cretan War (1645–69). Exhibits include a large, detailed model of Candia (as Iraklíon was then known) with 40 spotlights indicating the main monuments, and wall displays devoted to historic Venetian buildings in the city. Also new is the Ceramics Room, illustrating how pottery has evolved over 15 centuries. Outstanding examples of Byzantine art include a 13th-century apse fresco, one of the earliest to survive on the island, depicting the Virgin, St John, and the Church Fathers, Nicholas and Basil. One section is devoted to copies of frescoes from Cretan Byzantine churches, another contains liturgical objects from ancient churches now destroyed or converted to other uses.

El Greco

El Greco's painting of the Monastery of Saint Catherine on Mount Sinai, the only painting by El Greco to remain on the island of his birth, is given place of honour in its own darkened and air-conditioned room. This is no great masterpiece, but it is instantly recognisable as belonging to a different world from the precise Byzantine icons and stylised frescoes that hang in the other rooms of the museum. There is an impressionistic quality about the brushwork: note the marvellous economy with which El Greco delineates the travelling Bedouin and his camel. The swirling yellow-pink clouds suggest some divine presence in the heavens and Mount Sinai seems to bend before an invisible wind. Altogether, the painting is suffused with a strange and unearthly light, suggestive of passion and emotion. The work betrays the influence of El Greco's teacher, Titian, who was himself one of the great Venetian masters who developed the use of light to heighten the drama of his paintings. El Greco – born in Iraklíon in 1541 and christened Doménico Theotokópoulos – painted this work around 1570, and it marks a major stage in his transition from the Byzantine to the European style of art.

First floor

Harrowing documentary photographs bring home the human heroism and tragedy of World War II and the Battle of Crete (*see p112*). The most vivid shows Emmanuel Katsenavas and his son facing execution for their work in the Resistance – brave men visibly flinching in anticipation of the bullets that will shortly end their lives. Two contrasting studies have also been reconstructed here – one belonging to Emmanuel Tsouderós, the Réthymno-born prime minister of Greece at the time of the Battle of Crete, and the other to Níkos Kazantzákis (*see p68*), along with a display of his novels in various editions and languages.

Folk art
The cases devoted to Cretan folk art are full of richly coloured rugs and beautifully embroidered bodices and waistcoats. One room is furnished as a typical Cretan home, with a beaten-earth floor, stone benches and clay oil lamps. You can admire examples of Cretan bagpipes and lyres, and a splendid wedding bread, elaborately decorated with fishes and fruits.

Odós Kalokerinov 7, opposite Xenia Hotel, west of the Venetian Harbour. Tel: (2810) 283219. Open: Mon–Sat 9am–5pm (3pm in winter), Wed open until 9pm. Closed: Sun. Admission charge.

View of Mount Sinai and the Monastery in the Historical Museum of Crete

Icon Museum, Agía Aikaterínis

Crete holds a very special place in the history of icon painting. It was to this island that many of the best practitioners of the art fled after Constantinople (modern Istanbul) fell to the Turks in 1453. The Byzantine Empire had been deeply conservative in all things, including painting. Artists jealously preserved antique painting styles and techniques, which they brought to Crete and selectively passed on to pupils who were organised into schools and workshops, often attached to major monasteries.

East meets west

The church and monastery of Agía Aikaterínis, now the Icon Museum, was one of these schools. It was founded in 1555 when Crete was under Venetian rule. At almost precisely the same time, Venetian artists, such as Titian, Veronese and Tintoretto, were developing the High Renaissance style. Many Cretan artists studied for periods in Venetian workshops, and it was inevitable that there should be some cross-fertilisation

between backward-looking Cretan icon painting and the Venetian avant garde. El Greco (*see p36*) was one product of the meeting of the two cultures, and another was his near contemporary, Mikhaíl Damaskinós, whose works form the highlight of this small museum. Little is known about the life of Damaskinós, except that he studied in Venice during 1577–82, and that the icons displayed here were painted after his return to Crete, probably in the 1590s, for the monastery at Vrontísiou (*see p82*).

Italian style

The *Adoration of the Magi*, by Damaskinós, is an icon clearly influenced by Gozzoli's frescoes in the Medici Chapel in Florence. The lavish use of gold and the stylisation of the mountains and drapery mark this as a Byzantine work, but the figures, their gestures, expressions and postures are far more realistic than is normal in the iconic style. From Botticelli's painting of the *Nativity*, Damaskinós has taken the idea of including himself in the picture; he is the crowned king in scarlet cloak, staring directly and

ICONS AND MIRACLES

Icons are no mere pictures – to the faithful, they have miraculous powers, being a medium through which devotees can communicate with the saint or holy personage depicted – hence the votive offerings placed on or near icons by people seeking a cure for their complaints. Copies of miraculous icons have the same powers as the original – hence the practice of mass-producing icons and the innate conservatism of the art – worshippers want a precise copy, not artistic innovation. Perhaps that is why Damaskinós reverted to type in his later work – discarding all that he had learned from Renaissance artists.

questioningly out of the picture at the onlooker – in this case a somewhat idealised and youthful portrait. The icon depicting *The Last Supper* shows the degree to which Damaskinós embraced the rules of perspective, using the architectural framework and the table on which the supper is served to give his painting depth. His Apostles are all individual people, with thoughts, ideas, and expressions of their own.

Back to Byzantine

By comparison, the four remaining icons by Damaskinós show a reversion to the austerity and stylisation that is more typical of Byzantine icons. Faces are standardised and serenely emotionless. Several scenes are depicted at once, instead of the painting focusing on a single key event. In the *Virgin of the Burning Bush*, the central image is a symbolic one: the Virgin is burned but not consumed, she passes the test of absolute purity. *Noli me Tangere* shows the newly risen Christ appearing to the Holy Women, while *The Nicaean Ecumenical Council* shows the church fathers meeting to settle fundamental issues of Christian belief. The *Divine Liturgy* shows Christ as the first priest celebrating Communion with a congregation of angels.

Plateía Aikateríni. Open: Mon, Wed & Sat 9am–1pm; Tue, Thur & Fri 9am–1pm & 5–7pm; mornings only in winter. Closed: Sun. Admission charge.

Today's icon painters keep alive a centuries-old artistic tradition

ARCHÁNES

A good half day can be spent exploring the Minoan sites in and around Archánes, a prosperous agricultural town in the plain south of Iraklíon, renowned for the quality of its grapes. These are blessed in a festival that takes place every 6 August, following a custom that dates back, perhaps, to Minoan times, whereby the first fruits of the harvest are offered to the gods.

Archánes is, in fact, two villages rather than one. Shortly after entering the first part, Páno Archánes, park in the main square with its walnut trees, shops, church and war memorial.

Panagía Vatiótissa Church

The little triple-naved church with its baroque belltower contains a surprisingly rich collection of icons, many dating from the 16th and 17th centuries. One shows the popular Cretan theme of the *Virgin as the Fount of Life* – the Virgin and Child stand in a fountain from which miracle-working waters flow.

Minoan Archánes

The scant remains of Minoan Archánes are not signposted, but are easy to find. Walk up the square, towards the fork where the one-way system begins. Take the left fork, then first left. Turn left at the end of the street, then right. The next track on the right will take you to the locked gates of the site where you can glimpse the massive blocks of well-shaped masonry forming the theatre area, archive and reservoir of a major Minoan palace. The stone has turned pink from the fierce heat of the fire that

The baroque belltower of Panagía Vatiótissa church in Archánes

destroyed the palace in 1450 BC. Return to the main square, past houses built out of recycled Minoan masonry!

Fourní

Archaeologists cannot explore the palace site further because it lies beneath the modern town. They have, however, uncovered the huge cemetery at Fourní, on the town's outskirts. Reaching the site involves a long hard climb up a hill carpeted in wildflowers in spring.

Go back to the church and drive a short way out of the town, turn left by the large school and follow the signposted track until it ends; then follow the very steep track uphill to reach the site fence, following it to the left until you come to the entrance (normally open 8.30am–3pm).

Whether you think the effort of getting there worthwhile depends on your attitude to views. Set on a rocky plateau high above the town, the views stretch endlessly across the fertile plain that underpinned Minoan prosperity.

The most impressive tomb on this site lies some distance to the left of the entrance. Tholos Tomb A has a ceremonial approach ramp leading to the narrow entrance of a huge beehive-shaped chamber which must once have been visible from all over the valley. Archaeologists found the undisturbed remains of a princess, still wearing her jewellery, here.

Archánes Archaeological Museum

To learn more about the cemetery, it is worth visiting this excellent new museum. Go back to the town, follow the one-way system until you reach a large café-lined square where you can park, and walk, following signs to the museum. One of the principal exhibits here is a vivid reconstruction of the so-called human-sacrifice shrine at Anemóspili, 3km (2 miles) northwest of Archánes. Here archaeologists found controversial evidence that the Minoans practised human sacrifice. In this case a young man had been put to the knife in a last desperate attempt to avert the disastrous earthquake of 1700 BC which, minutes later, destroyed not just the shrine, but all the palaces on Crete, marking the end of the Old Palace period.

Open: daily 8.30am–3pm.

Vathýpetro

Today the Anemóspili shrine is no more than a platform of stone (surrounded by a stinking landfill site), and not really worth a visit. Far more rewarding is the Minoan villa at Vathýpetro, 5km (3 miles) south of Archánes. This idyllic site is surrounded by vineyards, just as it was in the period 1700–1450 BC when the villa was in use. The state of preservation is outstanding – you can even visit the original wine-making room with its clay presses and pans set out as if ready for the grape harvest to begin.

Open: 8.30am–3pm, except Mon.

Archánes is 16km (10 miles) south of Iraklíon.

Vineyards and olive groves dot the landscape at Vathýpetro

Enjoy a coffee by the waterfront in Ágios Nikólaos

ÁGIOS NIKÓLAOS

Ágios Nikólaos is one of the busiest tourist centres on Crete and, though tourism has swamped most traces of Cretan character, the town is still well worth a visit.

Mirabéllo Bay (Kolpos Mirampéllou)

Ágios Nikólaos sits on Mirabéllo Bay, the Bay of the Beautiful View, so-named by the Venetians who built a harbour here in the 13th century. Well protected from the prevailing westerly winds, the mirror-like surface of the bay contributes to the town's appeal, and there is a long waterfront promenade running north from the harbour along which to stroll and enjoy the views.

Lake Voulisméni

Right in the heart of the town is another stretch of water – the almost perfectly circular Lake Voulisméni, surrounded on its western side by high creeper-clad cliffs, and on its eastern side by pavement cafés positioned to take advantage of the lake views. So deep is the lake in proportion to its circumference that it was once thought to be bottomless. In fact, it is now known to be 64m (210ft) deep at the centre, with steeply sloping sides. Small boats can pass between the lake and the sea thanks to a channel dug in 1867–71.

Alongside this channel is the town's original harbour where glass-bottomed boats and luxury motor cruisers offer trips to Spinalónga Island (*see p76*), or night-time tours of the bay with dinner and Greek dancing. Running southwest from the harbour are the town's principal shopping streets, Odós 28 Octóbriou, and Odós Roussou Koundoúrou (*see p152*).

Archaeological Museum

The town's archaeological museum is just out of the centre, on the steep Odós Paleológou. Here, the origins of Minoan culture are particularly well represented, with good examples of neolithic and pre-palatial Minoan material on display in Room 1. Note the elegantly burnished vases with their long spouts and the stone phallus-shaped idol from a remote cave in Eastern Crete. The fertility theme continues in Room 2 where the so-called Goddess of Mýrtos is displayed, a bizarre early Minoan clay libation vase with phallic neck and head, clay lumps for breasts and a hatched triangle of pubic hair. She is less appealing than the delicate vessels made from marble and other coloured stones displayed in the same room.

Room 3 contains an exquisite stone libation vessel shaped like a triton shell. Carving such a vessel, using only primitive drills and abrasives, must have required exceptional skill and years of patient effort. The spirals of the outside of the shell are exactly duplicated on the inside of the vessel, and the whole surface is decorated with a scarcely visible relief of daemons making a libation.

After this masterpiece of Minoan art, the Dedalic-style figurines of later rooms, clearly influenced by Egyptian art, seem crude, and mass-produced, though the last room contains a macabre surprise – the grinning skull of a long-dead Roman with a funeral wreath of gold olive leaves garlanding his cranium. The skull came from a large Roman cemetery on the edge of Ágios Nikólaos. Placed in the mouth of the deceased was a 1st-century AD silver coin; such coins were placed in the mouth to pay the ferryman who, in Roman mythology, conveyed the dead to Hades across the River Styx.

Archaeological Museum open: Tue–Sun 8am–5pm. Closed: Mon.
Admission charge.

Ágios Nikólaos is 70km (43 miles) east of Iraklíon.

Ágios Nikólaos is full of life

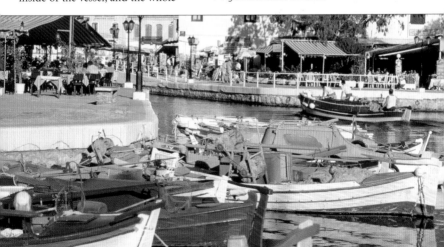

FESTÓS
Minoan palace

At the same time as Arthur Evans was excavating Knossós in 1900, an Italian team was busy uncovering the equally extensive remains of the Minoan palace at Festós. Evans' flair for self-publicity ensured that Knossós is now known the world over; far fewer people visit Festós. This magnificently sited palace is set on the flanks of a hill jutting out into the rich agricultural Mesarás plain. Archaeologists have argued convincingly that the palace was deliberately oriented so as to make the most of the views, and there is evidence here for gardens and water cascades, all of which must have contributed to the pleasure of living in such a fine spot.

Site tour

Unlike Knossós, Festós has not been reconstructed, and at first sight is rather confusing. Descending the path and steps from the ticket office, the palace lies to the left (east), while the jumble of walls, wells and circular storage pits to the right belongs to the Minoan town that clustered round the palace and cascaded down the slope of the hill to the plain below.

The West Court

The path brings you down to the West Court (1), with its raised footpath. From here there are good views of the imposing west façade of the palace (3), aligned to face the setting sun. In fact, two façades are visible: the monumental staircase on the left and the massive walls to either side of it belong to the New Palace, built after the earthquake of

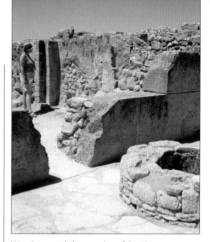

Wander round the remains of Festós

1700 BC. Running along the eastern edge of the West Court is the massive step-like plinth of the Old Palace façade, built around 1900 BC. Standing in the West Court it is clear that the remains of the Old Palace were levelled to create a platform on which the New Palace was erected. Archaeologists are still working on the southern part of the site to uncover more of the Old Palace and its associated town connected by a well-paved road. It is probable that valuable commodities, such as oil and grain, were carried in procession up this road to the palace, then brought up the monumental staircase (6) to the palace storerooms (9).

The monumental staircase

The staircase leads to a lobby marked by the base of a massive circular pillar (7). Beyond the lobby are the remains of a triple-pillared entrance (8) to a courtyard, or lightwell (a room open to the sky), from which narrow and winding passages lead left into the palace apartments and right into a massive stores complex (9).

Festós site plan

Key to map

1 Theatre area
2 Shrine complex
3 West façade
4 Ramp
5 Shops
6 Grand stairway
7 Propylaeum
8 Lightwell
9 Storeroom block
10 Pillared hall
11 Corridor
12 Lustral basin
13 Pillar crypt
14 Temple of Rhea
15 Peristyle hall
16 Lustral basin
17 King's apartments
18 Queen's apartments
19 Archives
20 Workshops
21 Furnace
22 Colonnaded court
23 Storage pits (cisterns)

Storage and distribution

Grain and oil were stored in large jars within the palace stores complex, the doors fastened with rope or cord to which a clay seal was attached to indicate ownership. Archaeologists found over 300 different seals, with designs ranging from animals to battle scenes and portraits. It is still not clear precisely how the Minoan economy worked, but the palace played an important role in the storage of valuable commodities – and perhaps in their distribution as well. It is possible that Minoans paid tax in the form of oil and grain – or that the ruling family was regarded as the owner of all the oil and grain produced by the community, or that individual owners entrusted their commodities to the palace for safekeeping.

Central Court

The stores complex runs along the west flank of the large Central Court, aligned to make the most of northward views to Mount Ida – and specifically to the cave at Kamáres, which was an important focus of religious ritual during the Minoan era. To the north of the court, the narrow entrance to the private palace apartments is flanked by sentry boxes. This corridor was open to the sky – hence the drainage channel to carry rainwater away. The corridor leads to the North Court, to the right of which was a small walled garden. To the north of the court, the Royal Apartments (17 and 18), also gave views – again to Mount Ida. On the far side of the Royal Quarters, down to the right, is a series of structures relating to the Old Palace, in

Symbol of wealth: oil storage jar

one of which the famous and mysterious Festós disc (now in the Archaeological Museum, Iraklíon) was found. The disc, of baked clay, is covered in indecipherable hieroglyphs arranged in a spiral pattern, perhaps of some religious significance.

Festós open: daily 8am–7.30pm. Admission charge.

AGÍA TRIÁDA

On the west side of the same hill on which Festós sits, there is another important Minoan site, Agía Triáda, traditionally described as a royal villa (for details of how to get there, *see p91*). Archaeologists are still not sure of the precise role of this building, or its relationship to Festós. It has been described as a rural retreat for the use of the Festós ruling family, and the very fine frescoes found here reinforce the idea that this was a place of leisured luxury. Also found here were the Chieftain Cup, Boxer Rhyton and Harvester Vase, the three famous stone vases, and the unique Agía Triáda Sarcophagus, all now in the

Archaeological Museum, Iraklíon
(*see p30*).

The idyllic setting of the villa adds to the notion that it was built for pleasure, for the building sits on a slope with views towards the glistening Mesará Bay (Kolpos Mesaras). It may once have stood even closer to the sea, for there is evidence to suggest that waves once lapped the base of the hill; silt deposition has pushed the sea back considerably over the last three to four millennia.

Site tour

Since the Minoan name of the villa is not known, Agía Triáda is named after a nearby church – but oddly enough, not the one that actually stands on the site: this church, Ágios Giórgios, nevertheless makes a good viewpoint from which to understand the site. Looking from the apse north to Mount Ida, the villa lies below, partly roofed over as a protection against rain. To the left are the private apartments, in the middle the storage areas and to the right the public rooms for entertainment and ceremonies.

Beyond the villa is the main street of a small town. Shops, all identical in size and shape, line the right-hand side of the street, fronted by a row of column bases that once supported a colonnade, perhaps to shelter market stalls. The presence of these shops so close to the villa is one reason for questioning the theory that it was a royal residence. Perhaps the whole site was a centre for large seasonal gatherings of some kind – for sport, ritual, song and dance, maybe? Only further excavation will reveal the truth. What is not in doubt is the ferocity of the fire that destroyed this building in 1450 BC – fire-blackened floors and steps provide a vivid reminder of the final fate of the Minoan palace culture.

Agía Triáda is open daily 8.30am–3pm. Admission charge.

Festós and Agía Triáda are 64km (40 miles) southwest of Iraklíon.

Agía Triáda: perhaps a summer palace or a cultural centre for sport, dance and song

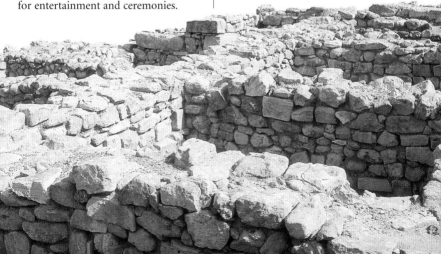

GORTÝS

When the Romans conquered Crete in 67 BC, the people of Gortýs took the side of the Roman general, Quintus Metellus. As a reward, their city was made capital of the Roman province of Cyrenaica, which also encompassed parts of North Africa. By the time of the Roman conquest, Gortýs was already an ancient city, described by the ancient Greek historian, Strabo, as having a wall 10km (6 miles) long around it. It was comprehensively remodelled along typical Roman lines, with baths, theatres, a governor's palace and a forum. The site today is massive, but only a fraction has been excavated. The Roman remains lie scattered across a huge area, with fallen columns lying among vineyards and olive groves, and Roman brick and tile littering the ground. After Saracen raiders looted Gortýs in AD 824, it was simply abandoned and left to decay because of the difficulty of defending the site.

Ágios Títos (Church of St Titus)

One building stands remarkably intact: the church of St Titus dominates the entrance to the site with its massive apse standing to the roof. The church dates back to the 6th century, and is the burial place of St Titus, the first bishop of Crete. Titus was sent here on a successful mission to convert Crete to Christianity after St Paul had visited the island in AD 50. It is quite likely that Titus would have made Gortýs his base, since it was then the largest city on Crete, with a population of approximately 30,000.

The 7th-century BC Temple of Apollo Pythios, with its stepped altar

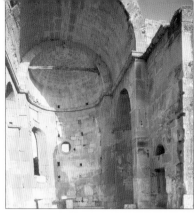

The 6th-century AD Ágios Títos church

Odeon – The Law Code of Gortýs

Emerging from what would have been the west door of the church of St Titus, you can see, over to the right, the impressive remains of the 1st-century BC Odeon, a theatre built for music and poetry recitals. The modern brick structure to the rear of the theatre shelters a remarkable 10-m (33-ft) stretch of wall covered in ancient Greek script, recording the Laws of Gortýs. Much of what we know about early Greek life and society comes from this important document, carved in sandstone, and found among the foundations of a pre-Roman building on the site of the Odeon.

The inscription reads from left to right and from right to left on alternate lines, in a style known as *boustrophedon*, meaning 'like the pattern made by oxen ploughing a field'. Though the inscription dates to around 450 BC, it probably records laws that had been observed for generations before – indeed, Plato, who mentions the code in his own book of Laws, describes it as a very conservative code. It divides the inhabitants of Gortýs into four classes – rulers, freemen, serfs and slaves – and describes in detail the rights of each with regard to property ownership, inheritance, marriage, divorce and the adoption of children, as well as laying down appropriate penalties for crimes such as rape, adultery and assault.

Temples and palaces

More excavated remains lie on the opposite side of the road. Turn left (east) along the Iraklíon road and walk for some 300m (980ft), ignoring the right turn to Mitrópoli. Look for a paved track on the right-hand side of the road that leads down to the Temple of Isis and Serapis, built in the 1st century AD for the worship of these Egyptian gods. To the south is the Temple of Apollo Pythios, a fascinating structure that may have been constructed as early as the 7th century BC and served as the main temple of the Roman city.

A track skirts the massive palace complex of the Roman provincial governor – the ruler of Crete and much of North Africa, responsible for ensuring a steady flow of wheat from these territories to other parts of the Roman Empire. Through the site fence it is possible to see beautifully paved courtyards, headless statues, fallen columns and numerous walls.

Open: the area enclosing the church of St Titus and the Odeon is open: May–Oct, daily 8am–7.30pm; off-season 8am–5pm. Admission charge. The rest of the site lies in olive groves and is freely accessible.

Gortýs is 46km (29 miles) south of Iraklíon, and 16km (10 miles) east of Festós.

Ruins of streets and workshops in the ancient Minoan town of Gourniá

GOURNIÁ

Gourniá is one of the best examples of an ancient Minoan town. It sits on a low hill near the safe anchorage of the Mirabello Bay, and the finds from the site indicate that it was a thriving industrial centre involved in pottery, metalworking and carpentry.

Most of the visible remains date to the New Palace period (1700–1450 BC), although there was a settlement here in the Old Palace period (from 1900 BC). The houses of the village were once several storeys high, and the very substantial walls that remain represent the basements, used for storage and as workshops, rather than the living areas. Turning left as you enter the site, you will walk up one of the main streets of the town, with its original paving intact. The street curves to the right and climbs to a flat area known as the Town Court. To the left (north) of this are the massive walls of a palatial building that may have been the residence of a local governor. The entrance to the palace site is marked by a flight of four steps. To the left of this is a huge stone slab, pierced by a hole in one corner. It has been suggested that this was an altar on which bulls were sacrificed; others have proposed that the slab was merely a butcher's block and that the Town Court served as a market place rather than as a ceremonial or sacrificial site.

Bearing left from the slab, walk downhill to the palace's massive sandstone east façade. Continuing down the path, ignore the first flight of stairs and take the second right which leads to a small shrine where cult objects associated with the Snake Goddess were found. From this point there is an excellent panorama of the whole site. *Gourniá is 90km (56 miles) east of Iraklíon, 21km (13 miles) southeast of Ágios Nikólaos. Open: Tue–Sun 8.30am–3pm. Closed: Mon. Free admission.*

IERÁPETRA

Ierápetra stands at the southern tip of a narrow neck of land where the distance between the north and south coast is a mere 14km (9 miles). There is little of interest on the broad flat plain to the north of Ierápetra, but wildflower lovers should look out for the entrance to the Monastiráki Gorge on the east of the road, a great cleft in the rock renowned for its plants. In Episkopí, 5km (3 miles) further south, an unusual 12th-century church lies almost hidden, below road level, opposite the unmissable, large modern church. Excavations have revealed that the church replaced an earlier one, perhaps 4th century in date, overlying a series of catacombs, or Early Christian burial chambers.

Ierápetra itself is the southernmost town in Europe, the biggest town on the south coast and a thriving tourist resort. Thanks to an earthquake that destroyed the town in 1780, there are few signs that this was once a Mediterranean trading port, particularly under the Romans. Displays in the small archaeological museum (*open: Tue–Sun 8.30am–3pm*) merely hint at the richness of the ancient town; important exhibits are the Minoan clay coffin, painted with hunting scenes, and the 2nd-century AD statue of the Roman goddess Demeter.

Down on the harbour, the restored Venetian fortress (*open daily, 9am–9pm; admission charge*) provides a more recent parallel for the earthquakes that destroyed the island's Minoan palaces in 1700 BC. In this case, it was in 1780 that the fort collapsed as a result of a massive earthquake, killing 300 men of the garrison. Just up from the harbour, signposts point to a house in which it is claimed (on very slim evidence) that Napoleon stayed one night in 1798, during his Egyptian campaign.

From Ierápetra, it is possible to take the south coast road east to Sitía, diverting after 21km (13 miles) on the new road to Moní Kápsa. The little-visited monastery of Moní Kápsa, founded in 1471, enjoys a spectacular coastal setting to the east of Ierápetra, and was largely rebuilt in the 19th century by Yerontoyiannis, a hermit who is revered locally as a saint, and whose body is preserved in a silver reliquary in the monastery church.

Ierápetra is 107km (66 miles) southeast of Iraklíon, 36km (22 miles) south of Ágios Nikólaos.

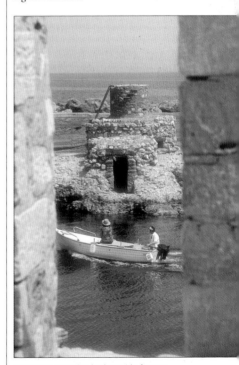

Ierápetra's Venetian harbourside fortress

Knossós

Knossós is one of the world's most famous archaeological sites and in high season it swarms with visitors. It is open for long hours, and a visit over lunchtime or in the early evening may prove more enjoyable than a morning visit when the crowds are at their peak. Allow at least two hours for your visit. (*See plan on pp54–5.*)

The palace of Knossós is part of Crete's early history

The palace

The present palace at Knossós is the last in a series of buildings on the site that date back to the origins of civilisation on Crete. Beneath the palace, archaeologists have discovered the remains of a neolithic settlement, dating to around 6000 BC. The earliest palace on the site dates from around 2000 BC. This, like all the other palaces on Crete, was destroyed in the earthquake of 1700 BC and then rebuilt in its present form.

Today, despite the collapse of the upper storeys of the palace, which were built of timber, stone and plaster, it is still possible to gauge something of its vast and labyrinthine nature. Only a fraction of the site is open to the public. At its height, the palace and its town spread over 75ha (185 acres) and had a population of around 12,000 – the same as Iraklíon in the Middle Ages.

Continuity

Unlike the other palaces of Crete, Knossós was only partially damaged by fire in 1400 BC. Indeed, it has been inhabited continuously ever since, and the present villages of Knossós and Makrítíchos (meaning 'long wall') lie on top of the Minoan town.

Even so, the site has been preserved in a remarkable state: wonderful treasures, such as the gaming board and the statue of the Snake Goddess, now in the Archaeological Museum in Iraklíon, along with bronze vessels, stone jars and the throne itself, were all found where they had been left. This suggests that, for centuries after the end of Minoan civilisation, the site was respected and not robbed – perhaps because of powerful memories of the myth of the Minotaur, the bull-headed monster of the labyrinth, who was thought to dwell beneath the palace.

Site tour

Visitors to the site are greeted by a bust of Arthur Evans (*see pp60–61*) who excavated Knossós between 1900 and 1906. The bust stands at the entrance to the West Court and, to the left, there are three huge stone-lined pits (1), probably built as granaries. At the base of the central pit you can see the steps and stone walls of one of the oldest stone houses found on the site, built around 2000 BC.

West Court

The whole of the palace complex served a ceremonial purpose, and the raised paths that cross the West Court were built as processional ways. Follow the raised path to the right of the Court and you will come up to the roped-off palace façade, clad in huge blocks of gypsum. This light and easily carved stone was used throughout the palace for cladding and paving. The use of gypsum for the façade would have given the palace a gleaming white, marble-like appearance.

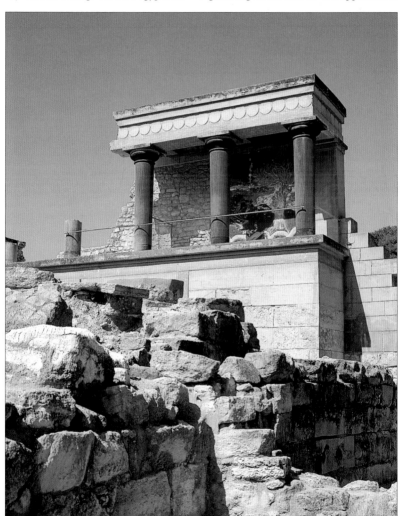

The restored North Entrance which originally displayed an imposing fresco of a charging bull

Key to map

1 Walled pits
2 West Porch
3 Corridor of the Procession Fresco
4 South Propylaea
5 Staircase to piano nobile
6 Lower storeroom block
7 Pillar crypts
8 Room of the column bases
9 Room of the tall pithos
10 Temple repository
11 Vat room
12 Antechamber
13 Throne room
14 Inner sanctum
15 Lower long corridor
16 Deposit of tablets
17 Lustral basin
18 Royal Road
19 Theatre area
20 Old keep
21 Northwest portico
22 North entrance passage with Charging Bull Fresco
23 Pillar hall (Customs House)
24 Corridor of the draughts board
25 Northeast hall
26 Magazine of the Giant Pithoi
27 East bastion
28 Court of the stork spout
29 Craftsman's workshop
30 East portico
31 Medallion Room
32 Corridor of the bays
33 East–west corridor
34 Grand staircase
35 Hall of the colonnades
36 Hall of the double axes (King's megaron)
37 Queen's megaron
38 Bathroom
39 Toilet
40 Court of the distaffs
41 Shrine of the double axes
42 Corridor of sword tablets
43 House of chancel screen
44 Minoan kiln
45 House of the fallen blocks
46 House of sacrificed oxen

Knossós site plan

Northeast
House

23

17

21

16

22

20

24

25

26

27

28

14   13   12

29

30

32   31

11   10
9

33

7

8

Central
Court

34   35

36

40

39   38   37

5

41

4

42

44

43

46   45

Southeast
House

0   10   20   30   40m

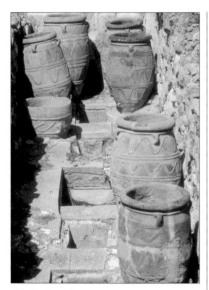
Pithoi in the palace storerooms

Corridor of the Procession Fresco

To the right of the façade is the West Porch (2), marked by a single central column base. Imagine now that massive double doors lie ahead. These swing open as we enter the Corridor of the Procession Fresco (3), so-called because the walls were lined on both sides with a frieze depicting hundreds of life-sized youths and maidens in procession and playing music.

The floor, still intact, is paved with sheets of blue schist set in red mortar. The corridor ends abruptly because the hillside has fallen away at this point; it once ran around three sides of a rectangle to return to the Central Court of the palace. To get there, turn left, then right through a reconstructed doorway into the paved area known as the South Propylaea (4). The pillared entrance to

the palace is decorated with a copy of the Cup Bearer Fresco, one of the best preserved of the figures from the Procession Fresco. Looking back, note the tapered red painted wooden columns that support the reconstructed doorways of the palace. The Minoans used whole trees as pillars, but inverted them, so that the wider root end of the tress was at the top.

Upper Propylaea

Beyond the fresco, the staircase ahead (5) leads to an area of the palace completely reconstructed by the excavator, Arthur Evans. It was his theory that the main reception rooms of the palace lay on this well-lit and airy upper storey. As you cross the upper floor, there are views to the left down onto the palace storerooms. Here you can see clearly the *pithoi*, giant storage jars, lining the long walls of each room, and then cisterns dug into the floor of the central corridor to create more storage space. We know, from Linear B clay tablets, that oil, grain, wool, dyestuffs and textiles were stored in rooms such as these, representing very considerable wealth.

Straight ahead lies a gallery where reproductions of the most famous Knossós frescoes have been hung, and through this room you reach a terrace. Turn left and left again to find a little staircase – one of many that must have provided a short cut from one part of the labyrinthine palace to another. Of equal interest is the fact that the walls containing the staircase are built on foundations from the Old Palace – hence its unusual rounded shape.

Central Court and Throne Room

The staircase brings you down to the Central Court, with the palace Throne Room on the left. In the antechamber (12) is a reconstruction of what Evans called 'the oldest throne in the world' – whilst the original gypsum throne survives intact, standing where it was placed some 3,500 years ago, in the railed-off inner sanctum (13). This Throne Room was in disarray when Evans excavated it, with jars overturned and littering the floor – enough for him to suggest that some dramatic final event took place here.

Royal Apartments

On the opposite side of the Central Court are the Royal Apartments.

This suite contains the most gracious rooms in the palace, many of them decorated with fine frescoes, such as the Dolphin, and the Girl Dancer Frescoes. Originally reconstructed by Evans as bedrooms, bathrooms and dressing rooms, it is now thought more likely that they were shrines, and not domestic rooms of any sort at all.

Waterworks and gardens

Continuing to the north of the site, there is a roofed-over area known as the Magazine of the Giant Pithoi (26), part of the room dating to the Old Palace period, and therefore almost 4,000 years old. Just in front of the magazine, steps descend right down to the palace east

Minoan murals adorn the inner walls of the Central Court

Large stone paved courtyards remain from the Palace of Knossós

entrance. Lining the staircase is a little water channel, with miniature rills (furrows to make the water ripple as it flows) and cascades. Anyone entering the palace on this side would have been greeted by the gentle sound of running water. Returning past the giant *pithoi*, to the top of the steps straight ahead, you reach a paved area with floor grilles: here are terracotta pipes from the original palace water supply, and stone drainage channels to carry rainwater away. A covered room to the left is known as the Medallion Room (31) because of the medallion-like circles applied as decoration to the giant storage jars found here. A staircase alongside brings you back to the Central Court.

Charging bulls and lustral basins

The north side of the Central Court is dominated by the imposing reproduction of the Charging Bull Fresco (22). Anyone entering the palace from the north side would have been greeted by this intimidating fresco, thought to have been part of a larger bull-leaping frieze. To the west of this can be seen a reconstructed lustral basin (17), consisting of steps leading down to the area where visitors were expected to wash and anoint themselves with oil.

The Theatre Area

Going west again is an area enclosed on two sides by steps (19). These have been interpreted as seating for the audience at some kind of sport or ritual, but alternative theories abound – more plausible is the idea that important guests were greeted here and, perhaps, entertained, before proceeding to the lustral basin for anointing and washing and from there on into the palace. This explanation seems correct in view of the fact that the Theatre Area stands at the end of the so-called Royal Road (18). This wide and well-paved street connects the palace with the vast town that once surrounded it and with Festós to the south. It has the distinction of being the oldest paved road in Europe.

Knossós, tel: (2810) 231940, is 5km (3 miles) south of Iraklíon. Open: daily May–Oct 8am–7.30pm, Nov–Apr 8am–5pm. Admission charge.

The impressive palace of Knossós, reminder of an ancient civilisation

Arthur Evans

Arthur John Evans was born in 1851, the son of Sir John Evans, a paper manufacturer and amateur archaeologist of Welsh descent. His father's interest became a passion with him, and he was largely responsible for the excavations of the capital of the Minoan civilisation, which he not only discovered, but substantially reconstructed.

A bust of Sir Arthur John Evans features prominently at the entrance to Knossós, paying tribute to a man who is something of a hero to the Cretans, as he should be, given how much Knossós earns in tourist revenue. Evans is less of a hero to the archaeological establishment, criticised for his intuitive reconstruction of frescoes and rooms in the palace: Logan Pearsall Smith, in a letter to Bernhard Berenson, wrote in 1926 that 'Evans is repainting and reconstructing Knossós in a gaudy style of bad taste which gives it something of the look of his hideous house in Boar's Hill'.

Controversial figure

Few visitors today would agree with this harsh judgement, but it remains fashionable to find fault with Evans' theories and interpretations, just as it was in his own time.

Evans sometimes invited criticism because of his own strength of character and his possessive attitude to all things Minoan. He was, after all, the owner of Knossós, having purchased the site in 1894, and used his own private fortune to fund the excavations. Ownership of the site was conveyed to the British School at Athens in 1924, and was then transferred to the Greek government in 1952.

The discovery of the Minoans

Evans began digging in 1900, making sensational discoveries almost every day, discoveries that were reported with astonishment in newspapers all over Europe, as the history of the ancient world was completely rewritten.

Linear A and B

Evans' name has become inextricably linked with the Minoans, but many other archaeologists have worked on the island, and continue to do so. The palace of Zákros was only discovered in 1961 and several sites are under excavation now, including the peripheral areas at Knossós. This work has added immensely to our knowledge of the Minoans, but their language and script – known as Linear A – have not yet been deciphered, despite enormous efforts on the part of many scholars. Linear A was in use from around 1650 BC but was superseded, after the final destruction of the New Palaces in 1450 BC, by the Mycenaean-influenced Linear B – a script that has been deciphered in part, yielding a great deal of information about the Minoan economy, but at a time when Minoan civilisation was a shadow of its former glory.

Abiding mysteries

The other great unsolved mystery is the precise cause of the fires that destroyed the Minoan palaces in 1450 BC. Evans' theory that the eruption of Théra, a whole half century earlier, caused the calamity is no longer believed. Many alternative theories exist, none of them borne out by the evidence – but there is increasing support for the idea that a major exodus occurred after 1450, with the Minoans, expert seafarers, fleeing their island and migrating all over Europe to found new cultures. The Etruscans of ancient Italy and the Philistines of ancient Palestine are among the peoples whose ceramics, jewellery and bronze-work bear a striking and intriguing similarity to that of the Minoans. Evans was knighted for his services to archaeology. He died in 1941.

Evans' bust at Knossós (facing page) and finds from the Knossós palace (above)

KRITSÁ
The church

The church of Panagía Kerá (Our Lady of Kerá) stands on the right-hand (northern) side of the road just before the village of Kritsá, usually unmissable because of the large number of tour buses parked alongside. This tiny domed church is one of the most rewarding sights on Crete and by far the best on the island for Byzantine wall paintings.

The church has a complex chronology that begins with the construction of the central nave and apse in the mid-13th century, not long after the Venetian occupation of Crete. The earliest paintings are those of the apse, followed by those paintings of the dome and nave. Next comes the south aisle (early 14th century), and finally the north aisle (mid-14th century). All the paintings have been restored, and are remarkable for the vividness of their colour and bold composition.

The apse

The oldest paintings in the church are those of the apse. Here, the *Ascension*,

Panagía Kerá church, covered inside with glowing Byzantine frescoes

on the ceiling, survives only as fragments, but saints Nicholas, Chrysostom, Basil and Gregory, dressed in priestly vestments covered with crosses and holding scrolls, are depicted in fine and intricate detail around the walls; the furrowed brows of the saints, and their intense gaze, helps convey a sense of exceptional wisdom and holiness, and suggests that these holy men are in deep contemplation of the eternal mysteries.

The dome and nave

Next in date comes the dome, where four scenes from the Bible are illustrated: *Christ's Presentation in the Temple*, his *Baptism*, the *Raising of Lazarus* and his *Entry into Jerusalem on Palm Sunday*. Other scenes on the nave walls and vault include a charming Nativity and a gruesome *Massacre of the Innocents* on the south side. On the opposite side, the *Last Supper* shows a table set with fashionable Venetian glass. Another sign of Venetian influence is the very rare portrait, on the north wall, lower register (below St George), of St Francis of Assisi, a Western, rather than an Orthodox, saint.

The south aisle

In the south aisle, an inscription names the donors of the fresco as the people of the village of Kritsá and one Antonios Lameras. The vibrant scenes depict the *Life of the Virgin* with an unusual degree of realism. In one scene, for example, Mary and Joseph sit dejected with their heads in their hands, obviously having had a row; Mary has just told Joseph of her pregnancy, and Joseph has

Densely packed houses crowd the hillside village of Kritsá

misunderstood; a helpful angel is descending from heaven to intervene and allay Joseph's concerns about the Virgin's virtue. Another scene shows Joachim, dejected in the desert, fasting for 40 days in the hope that his barren wife, Anna, will conceive (note the shepherds with their stylish cocked hats). In the next scene, Joachim and Anna rush to embrace in a scene that beautifully expresses their joy at Anna's miraculous conception of a child who will prove to be the Virgin Mary.

The north aisle

The frescoes here depict the Second Coming, with a vivid portrayal of the Garden of Paradise and its bird-filled trees and rivers. The first to be admitted to the garden by Saint Peter (bottom right) is the repentant thief who died with Christ on the cross. Seated with the Virgin and the Patriarchs are the Wise and Foolish Virgins of the Bible story, carrying candles, and with resplendent jewellery and hairstyles. More sober is the portrait of the donor on the opposite wall, with his wife and child, dressed in fine cloaks and linen caps in the style of the 14th century. Alongside, on the west wall, the Archangel Michael is blowing his trumpet to waken the dead and call them to Judgement – another angel weighs the resurrected souls in his scales. The earth is personified by a crowned female figure holding a snake that is coiled round her head – a throwback perhaps to the Minoan Snake Goddess?

Open: daily 8am–5pm (till 2pm on Sun). Admission charge.

Kritsá is 80km (50 miles) east of Iraklíon, 10km (6 miles) southwest of Ágios Nikólaos.

LASSÍTHIOU

The Lassíthiou, also known as the Lasíthi Plain, is a large oval plateau, completely ringed by mountains, with some 17 small villages dotted around its rim. The villagers make their living from agriculture: apples, almonds and potatoes are the principal crops, and the plain is beautiful in spring when the fruit trees are in blossom. In summer, the fields are irrigated using hundreds of white-sailed windmills which draw water up from underground aquifers (for a suggested route, *see p88*). The windmills are a famous and picturesque tourist attraction, though it can be hit and miss whether any will be operating at the time of your visit.

The aquifers (underground reservoirs) are restocked by the heavy rains that fall from October onwards. Flooding would be a threat if it were not for the drainage channels that divide the plain up into a grid, resembling the squares on a chessboard. The drainage system was first installed by the Romans, but the present system, cleaned out and restored, was installed under Venetian rule.

Caves and farmhouses

Most visitors come to Lassíthiou for the Díktaean Cave at Psychró (*see p72*). A less crowded alternative is the Trapéza (or Krónio) cave, to the south of Tzermiádo. This was used for burials in the neolithic era (around 5000 BC) and later as a Minoan sanctuary.

Also well worth a visit is the **Folk Museum** alongside the church in the village of Ágios Giórgios. This occupies a genuine farmhouse, with low ceilings, and smoke-blackened beams, built in

Lassíthiou's canvas-sailed windmills draw water from underground reservoirs

1800. Beside the door is a loom and the family bed is built over the wine press. Simple handmade furniture is stacked against the walls, and the kitchen area has a quern for grinding wheat, a bread oven, kneading troughs and storage jars. Alongside is a byre for sheep and goats and a separate stable for donkeys, with saddles, panniers and ploughs of the working farm. A more spacious and modern house alongside shows how Cretans live today.

Folk Museum open: summer only, daily 10am–4pm.

Lassíthiou lies 60km (37 miles) southeast of Iraklíon, 21km (13 miles) south of Mália.

LATÓ

From Kritsá (*see p62*) it is a short drive to the site of ancient Lató. On entering Kritsá, follow the one-way traffic system to the right. On a bend, after 300m (980ft), a sign points right to the archaeological site. From here, a metalled road passes 3.5km (2¼ miles) through ancient olive groves to the site car park.

The site

Lató is a relatively late foundation for Crete, dating from the Archaic period (7th century BC), after the end of mainstream Minoan culture. As always, wild flowers and splendid views add to the interest of the site. As you enter the site gate, a red arrow on the rocks points you up and to the right along a pottery-strewn track to the imposing city gate, built of massive square blocks of solidified lava. A tiny entrance, just wide enough to allow one person through, shows that no invader could enter the city from this direction without the greatest of difficulty.

The *agora*

Beyond, the stepped main street leads between the walls of shops and workshops up to the *agora* (market place) at the top of the hill. From here, and from the theatre terrace to the right, there are almost limitless views of eastern Crete. The deep cistern nearby indicates the importance of a water supply in the event of a siege.

To the left, on a higher terrace, are the remains of civic buildings where the town archives were kept, and where a perpetual flame was kept alight as a symbol of the town's continuity and as an offering to Hestia, the ancient Greek goddess of the hearth.

Site open: Tue–Sun 8.30am–3pm.
Closed: Mon. Free admission.

Lató is 80km (50 miles) east of Iraklíon, 10km (6 miles) southwest of Ágios Nikólaos, and 3.5km (2¼ miles) north of Kritsá.

Stone benches surround the hearths where fires burned in honour of the goddess Hestia, Lató

MÁLIA

Mália is the capital of beach-holiday Crete, a small town that has been swamped by discos, bars, English-style pubs and tavernas that sell beefburgers rather than Cretan food. The reason for all this development is the fine sandy beach that spreads for some distance either side of the town. Despite its size, this beach can be very crowded, and there are more atmospheric places to swim, one of them being just 4km (2½ miles) east of Mália, alongside the Minoan palace remains. To the disco-hungry crowd who come to Mália, the fact that there is a major Minoan palace on the town's doorstep is probably a matter of supreme indifference, which helps to explain why so few people visit the excavated remains and beach nearby.

The site

The palace sits on the coastal plain within sight and sound of the sea, and bumps in the fields to the south indicate the presence of a large town, as yet little explored. French-run excavations are continuing, and informative displays are found at key points around the site, explaining the work in progress.

A striking feature of the palace is the sheer number of areas set aside for

Silent reminders of the Mália Palace

storage. Sunken clay-lined pits and barrack-like blocks, built from mud brick and with their wine and oil-storage jars intact, surround the central court, leaving only a small area designated as living accommodation. To the northwest of the palace (in the area known as Quartier M), archaeologists have uncovered a group of buildings used as the palace administration block. Clay tablets inscribed with inventorial data, and seal stones used to seal boxes, jars and doorways, have been found here in great quantity. As with other Minoan palace sites, the building clearly played a key role in the storage and distribution of goods, but we are no nearer to knowing whether Minoan society was authoritarian, with all resources owned and controlled by the ruling family, or whether it was based on a more benign system of communal ownership.

Palace open: daily in summer 8.30am–3pm. Closed: Mon from Nov–Mar. Admission charge.

Mália is 38km (24 miles) east of Iraklíon.

MÁLIA ENVIRONS
Mílatos
This attractive fishing village is set above a pretty pebble beach. Mílatos is mentioned by Homer as one of the Cretan towns that sent troops to fight in the Trojan War, and archaeological evidence suggests that the village has been continually occupied for at least 5,000 years. Legend has it that migrants from this village founded the great and famous city of Miletos on the modern Turkish coast. Though this may seem no more than a coincidence of names, archaeologists have, in fact, found Minoan settlement remains at Turkish Miletos. About 3km east of the village lies the cave of Mílatos, where in 1823 an estimated 3,000 Cretans taking refuge were besieged by the Turks. Forced to surrender and promised a safe passage, they were then massacred or taken as slaves. A chapel with a small ossuary commemorates the event.

10km (6 miles) east of Mália.

Káto Karouzaná
Káto Karouzaná bills itself as 'The Traditional Village'. Popular with coach tours, the village is really an excuse to persuade visitors to part with their money in return for handicrafts such as woven rugs and pottery (although handwoven and painted, the designs are not always traditional). Displays of Greek dancing and music are put on in the evening, and used by tour companies.

15km (9 miles) south of Chersonísou.

Lychnostatis Museum
This is located just off the National Highway to the east of Chersonísou, another busy package-tour resort, some 12km (7 miles) to the west of Mália. Guided tours take in a reconstructed Cretan house, windmill, shepherd's shelter, pottery, weaving workshops and an olive oil press. Wine tastings and an audiovisual introduction to the attractions of Crete are all part of the package.

Open: Sun–Fri 9am–2pm. Closed: Sat and from 1 Nov–31 Mar. Admission charge.

The striking rock-cut tombs of Mátala were also used as homes in the past

MÁTALA

Even if you are not a beach lover, Mátala's sheltered bay, sandstone cliffs and lovely sunset views will not leave you unmoved. Mátala also makes an excellent base for exploring the major archaeological sites of Festós and Gortýs. The beach is impeccably clean and local shops are very well stocked, as befits a village that has almost become a German colony (there are even fragments of the Berlin Wall hanging in the reception area of one hotel).

Archaeology

The cliffs to the north of the bay contain scores of man-made caves where hippies made their homes when Crete was first 'discovered' in the 1970s. The caves were originally excavated in the 2nd century BC to serve as rock-cut tombs, and some have ornate carved niches within. Today the caves are fenced off and can be visited 8.30am–2pm.

A little to the north of Mátala is another sandy beach, stretching south from Kalamáki to Kómmos. Kómmos is the site of the Minoan harbour that served Festós, and American archaeologists digging here in the last ten years have uncovered substantial remains of roads, warehouses, dry docks and temples, some of which can be seen through the site fence.

Mátala is 70km (43 miles) southwest of Iraklíon, 10km (6 miles) southwest of Festós.

MYRTÍA
Kazantzákis Museum

Níkos Kazantzákis is one of the few Cretans whose name is well known beyond the shores of his own island, though his fame owes much more to film versions of his work than to his actual writings. The Kazantzákis Museum in Myrtía attempts to fill out the very vague picture that most of us have about his life and work. The museum is located on the village square in what is claimed to be the house of Kazantzákis' father. In fact, it has been substantially extended to accommodate case after case of Kazantzákis memorabilia: books, stills from film and stage versions of his works, costume designs, and personal possessions, such as signet rings and fountain pens.

Kazantzákis (1883–1957) was born in Iraklíon and studied law at Athens University and political science in Paris. Fellow Cretan Eleftherias Venizélos (*see p100*) made Kazantzákis Minister of Welfare in his Greek government of 1919, but he preferred travelling to politics, and lived abroad for many years writing a series of poems, plays, stories and poetic dramas. His grandiose language is out of fashion now, and his work is little read or performed.

Controversial novels

Kazantzákis became widely known through the enormous success of *Zorba the Greek* (1946), which was turned into a popular film with a haunting theme tune starring Anthony Quinn and Alan Bates (1964). Controversy also helped to promote his name: *Freedom or Death* (1953), about the Cretan resistance to Turkish rule, and *The Last Temptation of Christ* (1954) were both condemned by the Roman Catholic Church for blasphemy. More recently, Martin Scorsese's film version of *The Last Temptation of Christ* ran into similar trouble, criticised for portraying Christ as flawed and truly human, rather than sinless and divine. Conspiracy theorists go so far as to claim that the Church prevented Kazantzákis from receiving the Nobel Prize for Literature when he was nominated in 1955.

Museum open: Mon, Wed & Sat 9am–1pm & 4–8pm; Tue & Fri 9am–1pm. Closed: Thur & Sun.

Myrtía is 16km (10 miles) southeast of Iraklíon, 11km (7 miles) southeast of Knossós.

Cretan liars

On the way up to Myrtía look out for the distinctive profile of Mount Yioúktas to the west (right) once past Knossós. The mountain, with its radar station, looks like a human face, with prominent brow, nose, lips and chin. Cretans have long believed that this is the face of Zeus who lies buried beneath the mountain. Other Greeks branded Cretans as liars for daring to suggest that Zeus was anything but immortal (see p73).

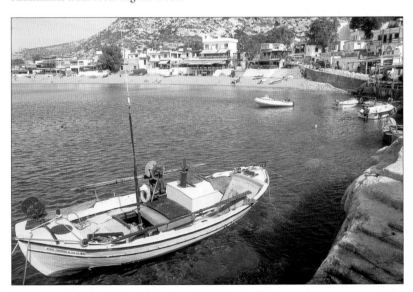

Mátala's west-facing bay is the ideal place to watch the sun go down

MONÍ TÓPLOU
The monastic complex

Moní Tóplou, or Tóplou monastery, sits on top of a bleak and windswept rocky plateau at the northeastern tip of the island, where few other people live. Tóplou is a word of Turkish origin meaning 'armed with cannon', and the monastery has been plundered and destroyed several times, hence its fortress-like appearance today. The monastery is immensely wealthy and the monks have restored much of the complex (critics say they have destroyed its character in the process), including a fine old Cretan windmill that stands just outside the monastery walls. This survives with its internal workings intact, providing a rare opportunity to see how the canvas sails turned the giant millstones within.

The gatehouse of the ancient part of the monastery leads into a delightful shady patio, paved with cobbles. Three storeys of monastic cells surround the courtyard on three sides, with a tall belltower, rising above the gatehouse, filling the fourth side. The tiny church to

Fortress-like Moní Tóplou

Moní Tóplou's pretty wheel window

the right has a pretty wheel window and four panels set into the façade. One is carved with a Virgin and Child in relief, dating perhaps to the 14th century when the church monastery was founded. Two other panels have inscriptions recording the restoration of the church after the 1612 earthquake. The fourth panel, a grey slab covered in minute script, dates from 132 BC, and records the so-called 'Arbitration of Magnesia'.

The rulers of the city of Magnesia (now in western Turkey) were called in to arbitrate in a long-standing land dispute between Ítanos and Ierápetra. The judgement (which came down in favour of Ítanos) was recorded on this slab and on a matching slab that still survives in Magnesia. Long after the dispute was forgotten, the slab was reused, first as a grave marker, then as an altar; its importance was not appreciated until a 19th-century Classics scholar, Robert Pashley, came across it when visiting this monastery in 1834.

Icons and engravings

The church contains a magnificent icon, called *Lord, thou art Great* because each of the 61 tiny scenes packed into the painting illustrates a line from this Greek Orthodox prayer. The scenes sum up the whole biblical story, from Creation to the Last Judgement, with especially lively depictions of the Story of Noah, Jonah and the Whale and the Destruction of the Cities of the Plain. A museum to the rear of the church contains more icons, but none as riveting as this one.

Another museum across the courtyard is devoted to 19th-century engravings of Mount Athos, once made by the monks to sell as souvenirs. A tiny room to one side of the museum is devoted to the monastery's role in the Cretan struggle for independence against the Turks and during World War II, when the abbot was executed for assisting the Resistance.
Open: daily 8am–1pm & 2–6pm. Admission charge.

Moní Tóplou is 150km (93 miles) east of Iraklíon, 14km (9 miles) east of Sitía.

MONÍ TÓPLOU ENVIRONS
Palm Beach

From Moní Tóplou a scenic road runs north through a bare upland landscape populated only by hardy sheep and goats. Just when you have convinced yourself that nothing could grow here except the most hardy of shrubs, you encounter beautiful groves of date palms at Váï. These are a distinct species of palm, known only on eastern Crete, and recorded as early as Roman times. They have given their name to the so-called Palm Beach at Váï, a lovely, but often very crowded, stretch of white sand. Just 2km (1¼ miles) to the north are the excavated ruins of the hilltop city of Ítanos, once an important harbour involved in trade with Egypt and the Near East.

Another important archaeological site is the ancient Minoan town Palecastro, some 8km (5 miles) south of Váï. There is little to see here at present, but recent field surveys suggest that the town was second only in size to that at Knossós, with the potential to yield much information about life for ordinary people in Minoan Crete.

Palm Beach is rarely so uncrowded

The view from the Díktaean Cave over the
Lassíthiou Plain

Psychró and the Díktaean Cave

The great god Zeus, destined to become
the supreme deity and ruler of the
heavens, was born in the Díktaean Cave
at some time back in the mists of
antiquity (*see p34*). Today, that cave is
one of the major tourist attractions on
Crete, but it is difficult to find awe and
reverence among the crowds who throng
the cave.

Practicalities

The cave entrance lies above the village
of Psychró, a village almost entirely
given over to the feeding of coach-borne
visitors to the cave and to the sale of
souvenirs. The cave entrance is a steep
15-minute climb up a well-trodden
path. You can travel up on the back of a
donkey, in true Cretan peasant style, if
you prefer.

This is one of the few places on Crete
where you are likely to encounter heavy
sales technique. Hawkers pester visitors
with offers of guided tours, and you may
even be told that hiring a guide is
compulsory: it is not, and it is entirely

up to you whether you want someone to
accompany you and point out the
principal features of the cave.

The cave itself echoes to the anxious
chatter of ill-equipped visitors
frightened that they are going to slip on
the damp rock of the steeply descending
cave footpath, or lose their way in the
gloom. The lesson of all this is to come
prepared – a torch is very useful, as are
non-slip shoes and a sweater against the
cold of the cave interior. You can enjoy a
degree of privacy by coming early in the
morning or in the late afternoon,
avoiding the worst of the coach tours
that congregate here in the hour or so
before and after lunch.

The cave

The Díktaean Cave is located in the
northern flanks of the Díkte mountain
range (Órosira Díkti) at an altitude of
1,025m (3,363ft). The cave consists of a
vast cavern, some 15m (49ft) high and
85m (279ft) deep. At the lowest section
there is a small pool and a number of
stalagmites that divide this part of the
cave into smaller chambers. Guides will
tell you that the stalagmite column to
the right of the pool represents Zeus's
Mantle, and that it was here that the
infant Zeus was fed by nymphs on wild
honey and goat's milk, while the
chamber to the left is the one where
Zeus was born.

The same chamber is where, in
1899–1900, archaeologists found the
greatest concentration of votive
offerings, including bronze and clay
figurines, gold brooches and bronze
axes, miniature versions of the sacred
Minoan *labrys*, or double-bladed axe.

These offerings had been thrown into the pool or placed in crevices and cracks around the cave wall and on the stalagmites. Most corresponded to the New Palace period on Crete (1700–1450 BC), with another group of finds dating from the Iron Age (8th and 7th centuries BC), representing a revival in the use of the cave for religious ritual. Higher up in the cave, nearer to the entrance, libation tables and altars were found along with the bones of sacrificial animals.

The legend of Zeus

Like other large caves on Crete, this was regarded as a holy place. Whether or not it really is the cave referred to in ancient myth as the birthplace of Zeus is a subject still debated by scholars. Epimenides, the poet born on Crete sometime in the 6th or 7th centuries BC, at about the time when the cult of Zeus was being revived, felt inclined to disbelieve the claims of his own countrymen. Indeed, he was the poet who famously branded all Cretans as liars (*see p69*), adding that they were 'noxious beasts' and 'evil bellies'. St Paul was later to quote these same words in writing to his follower, Titus, who was sent to Crete to convert the islanders to Christianity around AD 50. The reason for this disapproval was the Cretan belief that Zeus (regarded by Greeks as immortal) was dead and lay buried beneath Mount Yioúktas (*see p69*).

Cretans have a simple answer to this accusation: their Zeus is a different one from the Greek Zeus; the Cretan Zeus, worshipped as far back as neolithic times, was a vegetation god who died and rose again annually, rather than the Greek Zeus, the immortal sky god, who has attributes more in common with Oriental and Egyptian deities.

The Díktaean Cave is 2km (1¼ miles) south of the village. Open: daily 8am–6.45pm in summer; shorter hours in winter. Admission charge.

Psychró is 62km (39 miles) southeast of Iraklíon, on the southern rim of the Lassíthiou Plain.

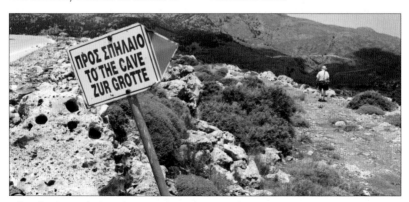

Follow the signs to the lesser-known Donkey Hole cave on the Lassíthiou Plain

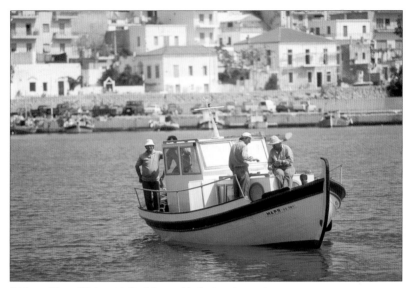

Setting out from Sitía to catch the fish served in the town's many tavernas

SITÍA

Sitía is the easternmost town of any significance on Crete. If you are interested in visiting this part of the island it makes a far more interesting base than Ágios Nikólaos or Ierápetra, having an easy-going but self-assured Cretan character, little affected by tourism. Tavernas are full of local people, and the food is of noticeably better quality than in the major resorts. No visitor to Sitía on a Sunday leaves without being impressed by the vitality of the evening stroll, the *voltá*, a legacy of Venetian rule, when just about everyone, old and young, priest and people, comes out to promenade along the palm-fringed seafront in their Sunday best. The town is worth a visit in August when the importance of the local raisin and sultana crop is celebrated

with its Sultana Festival. This is one of the liveliest excuses for song, dance and over-consumption to be found on Crete.

The sights

Continuing along the seafront opposite the Star Hotel are Roman semicircular rock-cut fish tanks. They are not easy to spot, being below the water line at times, and were once used for storing live fish until they were needed. On the hill is the square 13th-century fortress, the only evidence of Venetian occupation. This was reduced to a shell by the Turks and is now partly restored to serve as an open-air theatre.

The Folklore Museum is in Odós Kapetán Sífi, up from the harbour, and is notable for its collection of woven rugs, bed-hangings, blankets and baskets. The Archaeological Museum is to be found in the unpromising location of an industrial estate on the Ierápetra road, sandwiched between a marble mason's yard and a graveyard for rusting and broken-down tractors.

Archaeological Museum

The museum is, nevertheless, well laid out and labelled. The star exhibit is a wonderful ivory statue of a Minoan youth, known as the Palecastro Kouros. This has been painstakingly pieced together from numerous scattered fragments. The fire-blackened ivory recalls the dramatic final events that took place on Crete in 1450 BC when many Minoan towns and palaces were destroyed in an inferno.

Among the other exhibits are a number of extremely rare tablets covered in the as-yet undeciphered Linear A script (*see p60*). Other rarities include a carpenter's bronze saw from Zákros, a clay wine press and a clay barbecue grill. The final section of the museum contains Roman and Hellenistic material, including some fine bronze fish hooks, nails and jewellery.

Sitía is 140km (87 miles) east of Iraklíon, 70km (43 miles) east of Ágios Nikólaos. Folklore Museum. Open: Apr–Oct Mon 9.30am–1.30pm & 5–8pm, Tue–Fri 9.30am–2.30pm & 5–9pm, Sat 9.30am–2.30pm. Admission charge. Archaeological Museum. Open: Tue–Sun 8.30am–3pm. Closed: Mon. Admission charge.

SITÍA ENVIRONS
Praisós

Some of the finds in the Sitía Archaeological Museum come from the Hellenistic site of Praisós. This is worth seeking out, especially in spring, when it is carpeted in wildflowers. It was a major town of the Etocretans mentioned by Homer, and the rump of the Minoan peoples who survived the conflagration of 1450 BC and who continued with the old religious practices. Defensive works can be seen, as well as one fully excavated 3rd-century BC house, with extant olive press, water cistern and mortar.

15km (9 miles) south of Sitía.

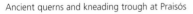
Ancient querns and kneading trough at Praisós

Spinalónga's fortress

SPINALÓNGA

The tiny offshore island of Spinalónga makes a popular excursion from both Ágios Nikólaos and Eloúnta. In both cases, tours depart from the harbour at regular intervals during the day, and the round trip takes about four hours. There may be an opportunity to swim during the trip and refreshments are served on the larger boats – otherwise, be sure to take something to eat and drink with you.

Spinalónga peninsula

You will see Spinalónga peninsula on the right-hand side (east) of the boat if you are travelling from Eloúnta, and on the left of the boat travelling from Ágios Nikólaos. The peninsula is known locally as 'Big Spinalónga' to distinguish it from the island, and it is attached to Crete only by a narrow sand spit. There is little to see here now of the once-thriving Hellenistic and Roman port of Oloús that stood at the southern end of the peninsula.

Spinalónga island

Spinalónga (which means 'long thorn' in Italian, a reference to its shape and pointed profile) is noted for having one of Crete's finest and best-preserved Venetian fortresses, built here in 1579 to protect the approaches to Spinalónga bay and the Gulf of Mirabello. Remarkably, it remained in Venetian hands long after the rest of Crete fell to the Turks in 1669, following the 21-year siege of Iraklíon.

Spinalónga was only surrendered to the Turks in 1715, and for several decades before that it was a place of refuge for Cretan resistance fighters, and for Christians escaping forcible conversion to Islam.

After 1715, Turkish families were settled on the island to prevent its use as a safe haven by Cretans. When the Turkish occupation ended at the end of the 19th century, the island was abandoned. From 1903 to 1955 it was used as a colony – in effect a prison – for lepers and others suffering from contagious diseases, a cruel and unnecessary practice. The island's lepers made what kind of a life they could among the ruins of the Turkish village, which remains a major feature of

Ayíi Pántes Nature Reserve

If you are taking the longer trip, from Ágios Nikólaos, the boat will first pass the offshore island nature reserve of Ayíi Pántes (All Saints), where the magnificently horned Cretan wild ibex is protected from hunting. Known as the *agrími*, or more popularly as the *krí krí*, this shy beast, which features in Minoan art, is all but extinct on the mainland. Small numbers survive in the Lefká Óri (White Mountains), but the main herd, some 200 strong, can only be seen (with the aid of binoculars) on this island.

the island to this day, albeit in a state of advanced decay.

ELOÚNTA

Eloúnta village has developed into a small and charming resort built around a harbour where fishermen can often be seen sorting and cleaning their catch and repairing their nets. Some visitors to eastern Crete prefer this quieter resort to the bustle of Ágios Nikólaos further south. To the south of the town, signposts pointing to 'The Other Side of Eloúnda' (*sic*) direct you down a long causeway to Spinalónga peninsula, with its walks, bird life and fine coastal views.

Magnificent views over the Gulf of Mirabello are also to be had from the hills surrounding the town, especially on the winding road west, signposted to Neápoli, which leads to the hilltop site of ancient Dríros. Here the remains of an *agora* (market place) and public buildings can be made out, including the footings of an 8th-century BC temple to Apollo Delphinios: though they may not look much, these remains represent one of the very first classical temples ever built in Greece, and are, therefore, of great archaeological importance.

72km (45 miles) east of Iraklíon, 12km (7 miles) north of Ágios Nikólaos.

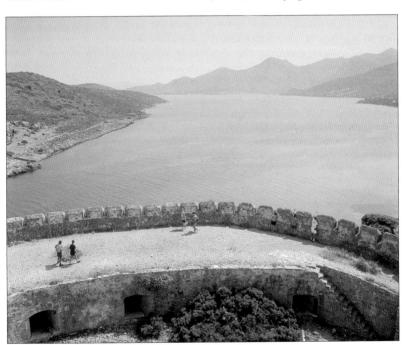

View from Spinalónga's fortress to Eloúnta

VÓROI
Museum of Cretan Ethnology

The area around Festós, in southern Crete, is well worth visiting for its major archaeological sites; another incentive to come here is the excellent Museum of Cretan Ethnology in Vóroi. This modern and sophisticated museum is housed in a building just to the south of the church.

Food from the wild

The displays here will answer a lot of the questions that any inquisitive traveller on Crete will have at the back of their minds. For example, what are the plants that the little old ladies, clad in black, are foraging for when you see them scouring the wild rocky hillsides of Crete. Case Number 1 provides some answers and covers the theme of foods gathered in the wild, from freshwater crabs and snails, to wild 'greens' (*horta* in Greek) – plants picked from the hillsides at any time from autumn until late spring and cooked by boiling, or frying in oil. The ingredients of *horta* include many relatives of the dandelion, as well as wild asparagus and artichoke. Once, such wild foods were a vital supplement to a near-starvation diet – today they are soul food for Cretans, evoking memories of the simple life of their forefathers, and the little old ladies sell the results of their foraging in local markets or to tavernas.

The farming year

The next run of display cases deals with the farming year on Crete, showing and explaining the various tools that are used at every stage, from tilling the soil,

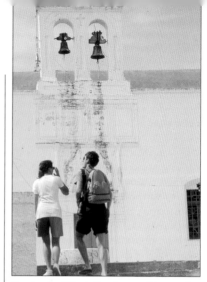

The church at Vóroi: though most visitors to the village make for the adjacent museum

to grinding wheat using watermills or hand querns. The exhibits include a vicious-looking plank set with sawblades and flints, resembling a medieval instrument of torture, but actually used for threshing grain. The operator stood or sat on the board while the animal pulled it round the threshing floor, the flint chips and saw blades breaking open the ears of wheat to release the grain. This, and the various ox-ploughs and sickles on display, are of a type that is quite likely to have been in use in the Mediterranean area from neolithic times until as recently as the 1970s and 1980s. Equally informative displays cover olive-oil production, viticulture and animal husbandry.

The enormous importance of sheep and goats to the Cretan economy is underlined by the displays on milk and cheese making, these two foods having provided the main source of protein in the Cretan diet for centuries. Meat was a rare luxury – sheep were kept principally for milk and wool, and cattle served primarily as draught animals; hens and pigeons supplied eggs, and rabbits and pigs were bred for meat. This diet was supplemented by hare, partridge and rabbit, trapped in the wild and once abundant on Crete.

Pottery and baskets

The ingenuity of Cretan potters is illustrated in the section on household vessels: jars for storing honey have a water trap around the rim to keep out ants and there are purpose-made vessels for storing pickled meat, salted fish, olives, oil, cereals, rusks, salt, water and wine – once the staples of the Cretan diet. Equally varied is the range of baskets (25 different types) used for harvesting and foraging, with marked regional variations in size and shape. Some baskets were used for storing grain, the inside having first been coated with cow-dung plaster and whitewash to deter weevils and mice. Pungent herbs were also placed amongst the grain to prevent meal worm developing.

Weaving

The museum's most colourful displays cover the processes involved in converting raw wool into richly patterned cloth. Wonderful examples of bags, towels, aprons, blankets and saddle covers are displayed, the likes of which are very rarely seen for sale in Crete today. Modern weavers still use the Cretan handloom, but their bright chemical dyes and leaping dolphin motifs are designed to please tourists – few now produce the traditional striped and geometric fabrics, in rich reds, greens and yellows obtained from vegetable dyes.

Museum of Cretan Ethnology. Open: daily 10am–6pm. Admission charge. Vóroi is 60km (37 miles) southwest of Iraklíon, 3km (2 miles) north of Festós.

Bright weaves typical of the exhibits at the Museum of Cretan Ethnology

The ruins of a Minoan palace, Zákros

ZÁKROS

Zákros is actually two villages, separated by a winding road with spectacular eastward views to the sea. Áno (Upper) Zákros is a relatively modern and prosperous agricultural town with little to delay travellers except for a few shops and tavernas. Káto (Lower) Zákros is, by contrast, a tranquil fishing village that feels as if it were at the end of the earth, sitting on its own sheltered bay, with a good shingle beach, at the eastern tip of Crete. Yet, in its Minoan heyday, this was the site of a palace as important as that at Knossós.

History

The town surrounding the palace was partially excavated in 1901, but only as recently as 1962 was the palace itself discovered. The remains, which lie to the rear of the village, are being excavated with painstaking care because they have the potential to yield important information about life in Minoan times. Much of the site is waterlogged, because the sea level has risen – or rather, the island has tilted – since Minoan times, and there is the potential to find important organic remains. It also seems that the palace remains were placed under some kind of taboo following the disastrous fire that struck here, as at other palaces on Crete, in 1450 BC. While parts of the Minoan town were reoccupied, nothing was touched in the palace, and archaeologists have even found intact bowls containing olives preserved as fresh as if they had just been picked, as well as numerous fine liturgical vessels and a considerable number of undeciphered Linear A clay tablets.

Trade with the East

Uniquely on Crete, this palace and town were built around a harbour, the remains of which now lie below sea level. Trade goods found by the excavators indicate that this was Minoan Crete's main gateway to the Orient, the point from which Minoan traders may have sailed to Egypt and beyond. Finds from the site include copper ingots identified as coming from Cyprus, gold and jewels from the Nile Delta, and both elephant and rhinoceros ivory, possibly from Syria. In return, Cretans would have traded dyed wool, metal vases and silver-inlaid cups; we know this from tomb paintings (dated 1520–1420 BC) in Upper Egypt depicting Minoan emissaries bearing these goods as gifts, and described, in the accompanying hieroglyphs, as 'from the land of Keftiu', which was the name that the Egyptians gave to Crete.

Workshops
Minoan Zákros was also an important manufacturing centre, and tools found on the site indicate that many of the rooms on the west side of the palace were used as foundries and workshops by pattern-makers, smiths, stone-workers and jewellers, potters and perfume-makers. Stores of unworked

marble and steatite, a soft carvable rock-like soapstone, were also found, and a marvellous vase, now in the Archaeological Museum in Iraklíon (*see p30*), carved from rock crystal.

The palace
It seems that the immediate environs of the palace were used by craftsmen working under the control of the palace inhabitants. As for the palace itself, it has a number of unusual features, including a unique circular chamber, fed by a spring, in the living quarters to the east of the court. This was surrounded by pillars to support a roof and has eight steps leading down into it. The chamber has been interpreted both as an aquarium and as a swimming pool – if so, it is the very first example of a prehistoric swimming pool ever identified.
Open: daily, summer 8am–5pm; winter 8am–3pm. Free admission.

Zákros is 170km (106 miles) east of Iraklíon, 44km (27 miles) southeast of Sitía.

The tranquil atmosphere of Káto (Lower) Zákros

ZARÓS

The large village of Zarós is set high on
the southern foothills of the Psiloreítis
range of mountains and is surrounded
by a cluster of worthwhile churches and
monasteries. The reason for Zarós being
located where it is becomes apparent if
you stop for a coffee in the village and
explore the pretty side streets, with their
colourful displays of pot plants. Water is
abundant here, running down the sides
of the streets and splashing into stone
troughs – numerous springs discharge
from the hills behind the village, and
in Roman times these were channelled
into an artificial watercourse and
carried to the town of Gortýs, some
13km (8 miles) south.

Zarós is 54km (34 miles) southwest
of Iraklíon.
Churches open all day. Free admission.

ZARÓS ENVIRONS
Moní Vrontísiou

To find Vrontísiou monastery, continue
through Zarós, turning right about 2km
(1¼ miles) west of the village. The
monastery entrance is shaded by two
giant plane trees, and to the left is a
small Venetian-era fountain featuring
the now headless figures of Adam and
Eve. Below them, water gushes from the
mouths of wild creatures with flowing
locks – possibly intended as lions. The
fountain probably dates from the 15th
century, while the monastery itself was
founded a century earlier, and dedicated
to St Antony, patron saint of hermits.
The double-naved church is full of
ancient icons, though the most famous,
painted by the great Mikhaíl
Damaskinós, are now in the Icon

Museum in Iraklíon (*see p38*). The
right-hand (southern) nave preserves
darkened 14th-century frescoes,
depicting the Last Supper (in the
apse) and scores of venerable saints
and patriarchs, representing the
Communion of the Saints, along
the walls. Coming out of the church,
do not miss the splendid views
over the Mesarás Plain to be had
from the terrace.

Varsamónero

To reach Varsamónero from Moní
Vrontísiou return to the main road
and turn right, continuing to Voríza.
Halfway up the hill in the middle of this
village, look for a blue sign pointing left
to Varsamónero. The bumpy concrete
road gives way eventually to a dirt track,
which leads for 2.5km (1½ miles) to the
church. This is set in a peaceful spot
alone among the hills. The exterior is
very simple – it has been cited as an
example of Venetian influence on
Byzantine architecture, but this runs to
little more than a hint of Gothic
dogtooth decoration and a carved
Venetian coat of arms over the
westernmost door.

This door, as becomes apparent when
you step into the church, leads into a
narthex, or antechamber to the main
body of the double-naved church.
The whole of the interior is covered in
richly coloured frescoes. The oldest are
in the northern nave; dating to 1321,
they depict the Life of the Virgin.
Within the lovely iconostasis (the
wooden screen carved with vine-leaves
that separates the nave from the
apse) there are scenes from the Life of

Christ, including his Baptism and Ascension, and his Entombment and Resurrection.

In the southern nave the frescoes, painted in 1406–7, depict scenes from the Life of St John the Baptist. Right opposite the entrance door is the scene in which Salome dances for Herod, while his guests tuck into a sumptuous banquet. In the next scene to the left, John the Baptist is beheaded. On the pillar behind these two scenes, the elongated figure of the Baptist with long and straggly hair has been compared to the work of El Greco.

In the third part of the church, there is a little apse set into the southeastern wall. The frescoes here, painted around 1431, depict Christ celebrating communion surrounded by a heavenly host of saints and angels. The remaining frescoes depict the exploits of the soldier-saint Phanourios, to whom this church is dedicated. On the opposite wall there are several further scenes from the Life of Christ, and a scene in which demons are being spewed out of the mouth of a demented man.

Visitors to Varsamónero's fresco-covered church will be enchanted by its rural setting

In AD 293 the Roman Empire, now so large that it covered almost all of modern Europe and the Near East, was split, for ease of administration, into eastern and western divisions. From AD 330 the Eastern Empire began to grow in stature when Constantine the Great founded the new city of Constantinopolis (modern Istanbul) on the site of a former Greek colony called Byzantium.

From Byzantium came the name for a new style of art and architecture that started here when the Church of the Apostles (now Ayía Sophia) was built in 537. Characterised by round arches, circles, domes and rich mosaic work (from which fresco

later developed), this style became the norm for church architecture in the Eastern Empire and beyond, lasting right up to the present.

The churches of Crete

Crete has one surviving church from the early Byzantine period – the 6th-century Ágios Títos, at Gortýs (see p48). By contrast there are several hundred churches and monasteries from the 10th

to 17th centuries, surviving in various states of repair. Some of the finest and most important have been restored, but most remain untouched, their frescoes cracked and blackened by centuries of candle soot, their simple walls leaning this way and that.

Most are simple churches with a nave, dome and apse. Separating the nave from the apse is an iconostasis, a carved and often gilded wooden screen on which icons (see p38) are displayed. The iconostasis serves to screen the altar since, in the Orthodox liturgy, key moments, such as the mystic transformation of bread and wine into Christ's flesh and blood, are performed in secret, away from the eyes of the congregation. Larger churches may have a second or even a third nave, each with its own iconostasis and apse, and occasionally a narthex, an entrance vestibule running the width of the church at the western end.

Frescoes

Frescoes are closely related to the architecture of the church. The dome, which represents the heavens, is usually painted with the figure of Christ Pantocrator (Ruler of All) looking down on the congregation, his hands raised in blessing and to display the wounds of his Crucifixion. In smaller churches without domes, Christ Pantocrator appears in the apse instead. In larger churches, the apse may feature the Last Supper, with Christ in the centre, or more probably the Communion of the Saints, with Christ as the officiating priest surrounded by angels, saints and patriarchs.

Many frescoes are also dated by an inscription, often located in the apse, or at the rear of the church, on the west wall. Occasionally there will also be a portrait of the donor and his family – look for this by the west door, or at the western end of the north wall of the nave.

Today's churches continue the style of their predecessors at Kanousi (facing page) and Episkopí (below)

Walk: Iraklíon

Despite its dusty streets and concrete buildings, Iraklíon remains a Cretan city at heart, with plenty of street life to make up for the uninspiring architecture (*for map of route see pp28–9*).

Allow 1½ hours.

Start at the Archaeological Museum. Walk around the western curve of Plateía Eleftherias.

1 Plateía Eleftherias

Pass the upmarket Astoria Capsis Hotel and several shops selling reproductions of Minoan pottery and jewellery. Irákliots still come to take coffee in the square, once the city's social heart, but huge tour buses calling at the museum have destroyed the former tranquillity. Turn right down Odós Daidálos to indulge in a spot of window shopping. Smart boutiques and jewellery shops line both sides of the pedestrianised street.

Head northwest up Odós Daidálos and turn right on Odós 25 Avgoústou.

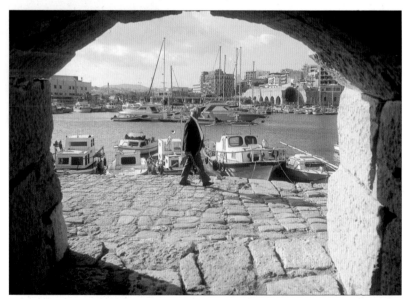

From Iraklíon's Venetian Fortress there are good views of the harbourside Arsenal and the city beyond

2 Plateía Venizélou

Plateía Venizélou is the city's other main square, lined with cafés, pastry shops and newspaper kiosks. The square is almost one large outdoor café and is liveliest at night. In the centre is the Morosini Fountain, built in 1628 by order of the city's Venetian governor, Francesco Morosini. The lower basin is carved with seahorses and cherubs, while the upper bowl rests on four lions, the lion being the symbol of St Mark and Venice.

Turn left here and cross the next road to find the city's bustling market in Odós 1866. This narrow street is lined with shops selling herbs, nuts, honey, embroidery, rugs, shoes, cheese, sponges and much more.

The fish market is at the very top of the street, where the aroma of coffee wafts from numerous cafés. One of these is set around a pretty kiosk converted from an old Turkish fountain, while behind is the Bembo Fountain of 1588 featuring a headless Roman statue from Ierápetra.

A walk through the fish market (in Odós Kartérou) introduces you to the many varieties of fish found in local waters.

Follow Odós Kartérou to Plateía Agía Aikateríni.

3 Plateía Agía Aikateríni

The peaceful Plateía Agía Aikateríni has three churches. The biggest is the ornate 19th-century cathedral. More interesting is its small 16th-century predecessor, alongside, containing an intricately carved iconostasis (1759) and charming scenes depicting Adam and Eve. On the

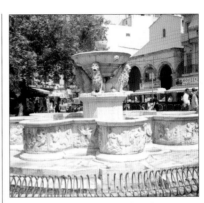

Iraklíon's market in Odós 1866 has plenty to offer

opposite side of the square, the church of St Catherine of Sinai (Agía Aikateríni) houses the Icon Collection (*see p38*). Follow the alley behind the church until it meets Odós 1821, then turn left back to Plateía Venizélou. Continue through the square, noting the Municipal Gallery on the right, housed in the church of Ágios Márcos, fronted by a 15th-century Renaissance arcade.

Almost next door is the Venetian armoury, now the City Hall, fronted by a Venetian loggia (arcade) of 1626 decorated with military emblems. Behind is the church of Ágios Títos, rebuilt in 1856, and housing the precious skull of the saint who was the friend of St Paul and first bishop of Crete (*see p48*). The skull is not on display but is occasionally brought out to be shown to the faithful.

Odós 25 Augoústou leads downhill from here to the harbour, and its imposing Venetian Fortress (*see p28*); the walk to the fortress and out along the sea wall is well worth doing for the views.

Tour: the Lassíthiou plateau

The famous windmills of the Lassíthiou plateau are highly photogenic, but increasingly rare to find. Even so, the plateau scenery certainly justifies a visit.

Allow at least 4 hours – all day if you plan to visit the Díktaean Cave (Diktaio Andro).

From Iraklíon head east on the National Highway (heading for Ágios Nikólaos). After 25km (16 miles) look for the right turn, clearly signposted to Kastélli/ Tzermiádho/Lassíthiou Plateau. This road follows the broad and scenic valley of the Aposelémis River to Potamiés.

After this village the hills enclosing the Lassíthiou plateau loom ahead like a cliff wall. Note the knob on the crest of the ridge, known as 'The Nail'. This outcrop was the site of a Minoan peak sanctuary where, intriguingly, the old religious rites continued to be practised for some 400 years after the final destruction of the Minoan palace culture in 1450 BC.

Progress is slower after the village of Goniés as the road begins to twist and turn. At the next junction turn right and continue upwards. Far below you will see the fertile Mokhós Plain. After 3km (2 miles) you will come to a side-turning (left) to Krási, worth a detour for coffee and to admire the massive plane tree on the main square while watching coach-borne tourists link arms to see how many people it takes to encircle the trunk. Another detour lies 2km (1¼ miles) to the right: **Moní Kerá** (Kerá Monastery) is largely modern but its hillside site guarantees sweeping views north to Día Island over the Gulf of Iraklíon (Kólpos Iraklíou).

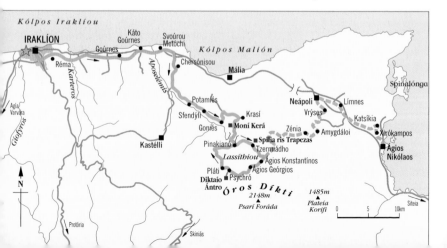

Shortly afterwards you will reach the Selí Ambélou pass (900m/2,953ft), where you can admire southward views that take in the whole Lassíthiou plateau. Rows of ruined windmills line the crest of the ridge to the east of the pass. Descending into the plain, the view ahead is of Psarí Fodára (meaning grey-haired female horse), at 2,148m (7,047ft) the highest peak in the Díktaean mountain range.

At the next junction you will come across extensively cultivated ground interspersed with fruit orchards. Huge rusting iron windmills are everywhere, but they look far from romantic unless you are here in summer when their canvas sails are unfurled to catch the wind (*see also p64*).

Turn left to begin a circular tour of the plateau villages. Tzermiádho is the principal town, full of old balconied houses hung with brightly coloured rugs and embroidery for sale. On the far side

of the village, a signpost points to the Trapéza Cave (also called Krónio Cave), site of recent excavations, and easily reached by a short footpath.

In Ágios Konstantínos it is well worth stopping to visit the clearly signposted **Cretan Folk Museum** set in a typical Cretan village house built in 1800. Psychró is a scruffy, commercialised village catering to the many visitors to the **Díktaean Cave** (*see p72*). From here the road continues round the plateau rim back to Pinakianó and Iraklíon.

Alternatively, you can continue your tour by backtracking through Ágios Konstantínos, and taking the right turning beyond the village for Neápoli and Ágios Nikólaos.

Moní Kerá
Open: daily 8am–1pm & 3–7pm.
Cretan Folk Museum.
Open: daily 10am–6pm.

The rugged landscape of the Lassíthiou plateau attracts many tourists

Tour: Cretan archaeology

This route takes in some of Crete's star archaeological attractions – the Roman capital of Gortýs and the Minoan palaces of Festós and Agía Triáda, ending up on the beautiful beach of Mátala.

Allow all day for the tour (with an early start) and consider spending the night in Mátala, then driving on to Agía Galíni to take the Amári Valley tour (p140) in the reverse direction to Réthymno.

Take the westward road out of Iraklíon, following signs to Réthymno. Where you meet the Old Road/New Road junction, 5km (3 miles) out of town, turn left following the New Road signs but pass under the highway rather than joining the sliproad. From here on it is easy driving all the way to Gortýs, but if you are planning to make this a two-day trip, you can make a two-hour diversion in Agía Varvára to visit Zarós and its churches.

Turn right in Agía Varvára to reach Zarós, a pleasant flower-filled village renowned for its spring waters. Continue through the village, and turn right, after 2km (1¼ miles), up a road signposted to the **Moní Vrontísiou** (*see p82*), worth visiting for its frescoes and views over the fertile Mesarás plain. Returning to the main road, turn right and continue to Voríza. Halfway up the hill in the middle of the village a blue sign points left to the **Moní Varsamónero**. Drive slowly down the bumpy concrete road which soon gives way to a dirt track. This simple church (*see p82*) enjoys a lovely peaceful setting.

Return to Zarós and, just before leaving the village, take the right turn signposted Moíres. This fast new road leads to Kapparianá. Turn left for **Gortýs** (*see p48*), the ancient Roman capital of Crete. It is tempting to explore for hours – though you should bear in mind that Agía Triáda shuts at 3pm and Festós at 7.30pm; so plan your day accordingly.

Drive west (signposted Vóroi) for 14km (9 miles) then take the left turn clearly signposted to **Festós**. You cannot miss the site (*see p44*): from the Festós car park head south towards Mátala, but turn right immediately beyond the end of the car park (opposite the little church that stands within the fenced

Festós is a feast for visitors in search of Crete's ancient past

area on the left). The 3-km (2-mile) track winds through countryside scarred by a forest fire and ends abruptly, with **Agía Triáda** nowhere in sight. In fact, the palace lies in pine trees below you and to the left (*see p46*).

Return to Festós and either turn right to descend to Mátala, or consider one last diversion, to see the outstanding **Museum of Cretan Ethnology** at Vóroi, which stays open until 6pm daily. To get there, drive back to the main valley road, turn left and first right into Vóroi, where the museum is in the village centre behind the church (*see p78*).

Mátala (*see p68*) makes a relaxing end to the day's excursion. If you are staying the night, aim to settle down into a west-facing café by sunset to watch the sun go down in a blaze of colour.

Western Crete

Western Crete consists of the two provinces (*nomoi*) of Réthymno and Chaniá, with populations of 86,000 and 156,000 respectively (42,000 and 53,000 in the provincial capitals). Both provinces are dominated by high mountains that rise gently from the northern coast, where most of the towns and villages are located, dropping very steeply to the narrow coastal strip on the southern side of the island.

Western Crete is a flower-lover's paradise

Beaches

Beach lovers looking for the choicest spots in Western Crete should consider the strip from Chaniá to Máleme, the lonely beaches stretching south from Falásarna and the idyllic coral islands of Elafonísi.

Mountain peaks

In Chaniá, the peaks of the Lefká Óri (the White Mountains) fill the horizon whenever you turn your eyes to the south. They are named after the snows that cover the long east–west ridge for six months of the year (November to April) and because the grey-white limestone screes that rise above the tree line look like snow during the summer months. This is serious mountaineering country, and those who make it to the top of Páchnes (2,453m/8,048ft) have been building a massive cairn on the summit for some years. Their objective is to erode the 3-m (10-ft) height difference between this, Crete's second highest peak, and Tímios Stavrós (2,456m/8,058ft), the island's highest peak, also referred to as Mount

Psiloreítis or Mount Ida, located at the western end of the Psiloreítis range in the adjacent province of Réthymno. Climbing Tímios Stavrós does not represent quite the same challenge since well-marked shepherds' tracks lead up to the chapel on the summit. Roads also penetrate a long way up the northern slope of the range to the Ídaean Cave, where Zeus spent his childhood, suckled by wild goats, and where Crete's first ski centre has been established.

Natural beauty

If eastern Crete has the lion's share of the island's archaeology, western Crete wins on natural beauty. The region has numerous deep, water-eroded ravines – not just the overcrowded and popular Samariá Gorge, but also the Thériso, Ímvros and Kourtaliotiko ravines (*see p126, p136, p144, p142*), the almost undiscovered 7-km (4-mile) long Agía Iríni Gorge (starting 20km/12 miles north of Soúgia), and the Arádena Gorge to the west of Chóra Sfakíon. This is also the richest part of the island for botanists, with far less soil under cultivation and a great range of habitats, from beaches and cliffs to swamps and river estuaries, where wading birds and terrapins add to the biological diversity.

Provincial capitals

Above all, western Crete has the island's two most attractive towns, in Chaniá and Réthymno, the provincial capitals. Both have colourful harbours guarded by fine Venetian fortresses, and are lined with cafés and tavernas. Réthymno perhaps preserves more of its Turkish heritage, with delicate minarets of golden sandstone soaring above the domed Venetian churches, and beautifully carved wooden balconies, typical of Ottoman-style architecture, projecting from upper storeys. Chaniá, by contrast, is more of a Venetian city, its narrow streets lined with classical palazzi decorated with wrought-iron balconies. Here and there, a narrow gate provides a view of delightful patio gardens or shady, flower-filled courtyards, and, also like Venice, sleek cats prowl the streets as if they were the true owners.

Orange groves

Travelling west, the national highway has been extended as far as Geráni, leaving only the stretch between here and Kolymvári to be completed. Inland, narrow country roads weave in and out of huge citrus groves. During spring, the scent of orange blossom is overpowering – the air is thick with the sweet smell, and equally sweet fruit that is ready for picking from late October. Green-skinned, even when ripe, Crete's oranges really are ambrosial, and one taste will make you realise why they are in such demand in the far-off markets of Athens. Away from this intensively cultivated part of the coastal plain there are some of the loneliest spots on Crete, and some of the least-visited and most unspoiled villages on the whole island.

A picture-postcard view of Réthymno harbour

Western Crete

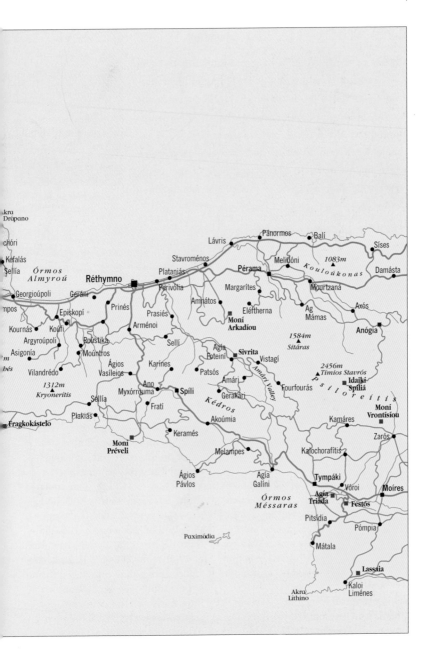

Chaniá

Chaniá easily wins the title of most beautiful harbour in Crete, lined as it is with pastel-painted houses with orange-tiled roofs, varied by the strikingly exotic domes of the Mosque of the Janissaries. Enclosing the whole harbour is the 16th-century sea wall, built of cream-coloured stone, leaving open only a narrow entrance channel through which boats slip, under the watchful eye of the solidly impressive Firkás (which now houses the Naval Museum – *see p98*).

Chaniá: perspective from the sea to the mountains

Despite such defences, Chaniá fell to the Turks in 1645, the year in which the Mosque of the Janissaries was built. The Turks made Chaniá the capital of Crete, and so it remained until 1971 when the title passed to Iraklíon.

The legacy of Venetian rule is visible everywhere in the city, from the beautiful town houses of the old city (*see* Walk *on p132*) to the massive Arsenal, or shipyard, lining the eastern waterfront. The Turks built their city, known as Kastélli, on the hill above the mosque. The massive walls of their fortifications are visible from the waterfront, but bombing in World War II destroyed most of the old houses. Excavations at the heart of Kastélli (left open and visible on the left-hand side of Odós Karneváro) have revealed the tantalising remains of a massive Minoan town, whose name (preserved in Linear B clay tablets) was Kydonia.

Archaeological Museum

Chaniá's Archaeological Museum is housed in a large but simple 13th-century church built to serve the city's long-demolished Franciscan friary, established under Venetian rule. The exhibits provide an overview of the type of material typically found on Minoan sites in Chaniá province. There are few outstanding works of art, though cases in the north aisle contain interesting fertility figures, and there is a toy dog made from clay that was found in a child's grave.

At the eastern end of the church are several statues and mosaics of Roman date, including an appealing marble figure of Aphrodite and some highly accomplished 3rd-century mosaics from a town house in Chaniá. One contains depictions of the seasons and another shows Dionysos discovering Ariadne on the island of Naxos (*see p35*), while a third, depicting the myth of Poseidon and Amymone, is enlivened by a little vignette of fighting cockerels at the top. Off the south aisle is a little garden littered with ancient masonry whose centrepiece is a ten-sided fountain dating from the Turkish occupation.

Odós Khalídon 21. Open: summer, Mon 1–7.30pm, Tue–Sun 8.30am–7.30pm; off-season, Mon 1–5pm, Tue–Fri 8.30am–5pm, weekends 8.30am–3pm. Admission charge.

Historical Archives of Crete

The little-visited Historical Museum is located in an elegant but faded town house in the city's early 20th-century southern suburbs. This area became fashionable from 1898 when Crete gained limited autonomy from Turkish rule, and when Prince George of Greece, appointed High Commissioner (in effect ruler of the island), chose this part of the city for his official residence. The relevance of all this becomes clear once you enter the museum, which is virtually a shrine to the heroes of the Cretan resistance and the political figures who brought about freedom from Turkish rule, and unification with Greece. Eleftherias Venizélos, for example (*see p100*), gets a whole room to himself, to the right of the entrance, and the downstairs corridor bristles with displays of the beautifully decorated swords and guns of Cretan freedom fighters.

At the foot of the staircase at the end of the corridor is the museum's star exhibit, a rare 16th-century cupboard carved in relief with hunting scenes. The stairs themselves feature grim reminders of World War II – a Nazi flag, an execution stake ominously hacked about at head height, and horrifying photographs of Cretan peasants and English soldiers bludgeoning German parachutists to death. Two rooms full of antique textiles and a magnificent

Locals and tourists congregate at the cafés by the water's edge

Chaniá town plan (see pp132–3 for walk)

Fáros

Ven

Ágios Salvátore

PLATEÍA TALO

Firkás (Naval Museum)

Telon

ODÓS THEOTOKOPOULOU

PLATEÍA MERARHIAS

ODÓS APOU MARKOU

Arcade of St Mark

OD ANGELOU

Venetian Palace

AKTI TOMBAZI

TOPANÁS

ATKI KANARI

Mosque of the Janissaries

KASTÉLLI

Minoan Excavations (Kydonia)

ODÓS PIREOS

ODÓS LITHINON

ODÓS APOSTOLIDOU

Reníeri Gate

AKTI KOUNTOURIOTI

ODÓS KARNEVARO

ODÓS SIFAKA

ODÓS APOU MARKOU

METAXAKI

Gateway

PLATEÍA SANTRIVANI

ODÓS

ODÓS PATRIÁRHOU NIKIOU

ODÓS ZAMBELIOU

Loggía

ÉVREIKA

ODÓS KARAOLÍ-DIMITRIOU

O NIKIF EPISKOPOU

ODÓS K

Archaiologikó Mouseío (Ágios Francíscus)

ODÓS PATRIÁRHOU GERASIMOU

Turkish Baths

ODÓS TSOUL

Katholikí Ekklisía

ODÓS KHALIDON

Church of Three Martyrs

ODÓS PIREOS

Schiavo-Lando Bastion

ODÓS SKRIDLÓF

O MOUSSOURON

Agorá

PARDALI

ODÓS MEL PIGA

ODÓS METAXAKI

PLATEÍA S VENIZÉLO

O KONSTANINOU A

CHATZI MIKALI GIAN

OD PLASTIRA

AG PERIDOU

ODÓS KIRILOU

ODÓS SKALIDI

O KARASKAKI

ODÓS KRIÁRI

PLATEÍA MAHIS

ODÓS SELINOU

ODÓS KORONEOU

ODÓS KÓRAKA

SARATSOGLOU

ODÓS DANAI

ODÓS MANOUSSOGIANAKIDON

ODÓS P. KELAIDI

SFAKIANAKI

ZIMIRAKAKIDON

PLATEÍA 1866

ODÓS MILONOGIANI

KIDONIAS

ODÓS KALISPERIDON

ODÓS KIDONIAS

ODÓS KISSAM

MARGONIOU

ODÓS IONIAS

Dimarcheío

Touristikí Astynomía

ODÓS IPSILANTON

nuptial bed are often closed but are well worth seeing when possible.
Odós Sfakion náki 20. Open: Mon–Fri 9am–1pm. Free admission.

Naval Museum

Housed in Chaniá's Firkás, this museum explains far more than the naval history of Crete, though models of ships, from

17th century, complete with its monasteries, synagogue, arsenal (dockyard) and fortifications. Alongside, a beautifully drawn map shows which of these Venetian structures have survived to this day – a surprisingly large number in fact.

For many visitors the upstairs displays on the Battle of Crete (*see p112*) will probably prove the most enthralling. The story of the battle is told in detail through contemporary photographs, newspaper reports, and war relics such as a spectacular wedding dress made from parachute silk.

Aktí Kountourioti. Open: daily 9am–4pm. Admission charge.

Maritime Crete at the Naval Museum

ancient Greek times until the present era, do figure prominently.

Of more general interest is the splendid scale model of Chaniá in the

Agía Triáda monastery

AKROTÍRI PENINSULA

The Akrotíri peninsula juts out like a clenched fist to the northeast of Chaniá, enclosing to the south the beautiful sweep of Soúda Bay, much of which is out of bounds to ordinary mortals, being the site of a large NATO naval base. The once-peaceful peninsula is now the site of Crete's second airport, and this has stimulated major development as factories and distribution warehouses are constructed to take advantage of the airport's proximity. Even so, there are some wild and unspoiled areas to the north, including Stavrós, a pretty fishing village enclosed by high cliffs, where the final scenes in *Zorba the Greek* were filmed.

The Venizélos Graves

If you drive east out of Chaniá, following the signs for the airport, you will climb for some 4km (2½ miles) until a sign on the left points to the Venizélos Graves. It was here on this hill, in 1897, at a very tense moment in the Cretan War of Independence, that Cretan fighters raised the Greek flag in defiance of the Turks. The flag was almost instantly demolished by shells fired from a battleship in the harbour below, one of which also hit the church. The ship that fired the shells was itself sunk the next day, an act of divine revenge, according to devout Cretans.

Among the partisans who raised the Greek flag on that day was Eleftherias Venizélos (1864–1936), a prominent figure in the War of Independence, who went on to become prime minister of Greece in 1910. He survived one assassination attempt and, in 1935, having led an abortive republican coup, was condemned to death by victorious monarchists. He avoided execution by fleeing to Paris where he died shortly after. To Cretans he remains a hero and an almost saintly figure. He is buried on this beautiful and restful hilltop site high above Chaniá, together with his son, Sophoklés.

If for no other reason, the panoramic views make this spot worth seeking out – additional attractions include a pleasant tree-shaded park (good for a lunchtime picnic) and the little Byzantine church of Profítis Ilías that stands close to the graves.

Agía Triáda

This 17th-century monastery lies 2km (1¼ miles) north of the airport. The sleepy monastic buildings show clearly the influence of Venetian architecture in, for example, the belltower that rises high above the entrance gate, and in the classical purity of the church façade. The church contains carved wooden choir stalls and there is a small display of

vestments, icons and illuminated prayer books.
Open: Tue–Sun 8.30am–3pm.

Gouvernéto and Katholikó

Keen walkers, and drivers prepared to take it slowly, can follow the track from the monastery that leads, after 4km (2½ miles), to the more remote Gouvernéto monastery. This dates from the 11th century, but is essentially a 16th-century complex, restored in 1821, with many fine Venetian-inspired details. Older still are the ruins of Katholikó, beautifully sited in a ravine 25 minutes' walk down the hillside. This was founded early in the 11th century by St John the Hermit. Hundreds of pilgrims come here for his feast day, on 7 October, one of western Crete's most important religious festivals.

Soúda Bay Allied War Cemetery

Another worthwhile stop is the Soúda Bay Allied War Cemetery on the neck of land just north of Soúda itself. Eucalyptus trees surround this peaceful and reflective spot on three sides, leaving open the fine views to Soúda Bay, a lovely stretch of blue water framed by peaks and dotted with the

Moving memorials to the victims of war

aircraft carriers of the modern NATO fleet. Here are buried some 1,527 of the 2,000 Commonwealth soldiers who died in the Cretan campaign; many of them are anonymous and marked by a slab that simply says 'Known unto God'.

The Akrotíri peninsula lies immediately to the northeast of Chaniá.

Despite the presence of the airport and naval base, the Akrotíri peninsula has its peaceful spots

The Ídaean Cave where, according to mythology, Zeus spent his infancy

ANÓGIA

Anógia is well placed to serve as a base for exploring the villages and sights that lie along the northern flank of the Psiloreítis mountain range. Part of Anógia's appeal lies in its reputation as a weaving centre; tour buses bring people here to watch weavers at work and to shop for blankets, wall hangings, and shoulder bags of brightly coloured woven wool. The town has a traditional air, but most of the buildings date from the post-war era: Anógia was destroyed in August 1944 for being, in the words of the German commander on Crete, 'a centre of British espionage and an asylum for resistance bands'.
Anógia is 35km (22 miles) southwest of Iraklíon.

ANÓGIA ENVIRONS
The Ídaean Cave (Ideon Andron)
South of Anógia, a steep and winding road heads south into the mountains to Crete's only ski centre, and on to the Ídaean Cave. Some claim that this cave was the true birthplace of Zeus (*see p34*), rather than the Díktaean Cave (*see p72*) which lies further to the east. Others say that Zeus was born in the Díktaean Cave but brought up in this cave. Certainly the cave has long been revered, and is mentioned in the writings of both Plato and Pythagoras. Archaeologists are working to find out more.

If you venture up here in summer, when excavation work is in progress, you can watch the painstaking work of sifting the cave deposits. Another reason for coming here is for the wildflowers: at this high altitude (1,500m/4,921ft and above), spring comes up to eight weeks later than on the coast, so you can see a mass of bulbs and other wildflowers as late as June. The high pastures also support seasonal grazing, and the shepherds still use the traditional circular stone huts that dot the landscape as places of shelter, and as dairies, where the animals are milked and the milk is made into cheese.

Fódele

Fódele is promoted as the birthplace of the artist, El Greco (born Doménikos Theotokópoulos). In fact it is more likely that he was born in Iraklíon, but this does not stop the village exploiting the El Greco association, even to the extent that his family's house has been identified and restored to pristine newness. The house is signposted from the village and delightfully located in an orange grove about 1km (⅔ mile) from the village centre. Opposite the house is the lovely domed church of the Panagía (the Virgin), built in the early 14th century but incorporating the nave of its 8th-century predecessor. The frescoes (dated 1323) are far from complete but have been well restored and depict saints, angels and scenes from the Life of Christ.

Fódele is 27km (17 miles) west of Iraklíon.

Tílisos

From Fódele, a new road leads north to join the Old Highway, now superseded by the New Highway running along the north coast. From here the best way to Anógia is via Tílisos, a town that, remarkably, preserves something like its ancient Minoan name – it is called Turiso in Linear B clay tablets. It is also the site of three large Minoan villas dating from the New Palace period (1700–1450 BC). These have survived remarkably intact – in the case of Villa C, the walls stand almost to first-floor level, with flights of stone stairs leading up to what would have been the living quarters. The villas have features similar to the great palace sites, such as lustral basins (for washing and anointing visitors), shrines, treasuries and rooms full of giant storage jars. Unusually, there are also rooms in Villas A and C with drains leading through the outer walls: these have been interpreted as possible toilets.

Tílisos is 10km (6 miles) west of Iraklíon. Villas open: Tue–Sun 8.30am–3pm. Closed: Mon. Admission charge.

ΔΟΜΗΝΙΚΟΣ ΘΕΟΤΟΚΟΠΟΥΛΟΣ
EL GRECO

Bust of El Greco in Fódele

The quiet beach at little-visited Falásarna

KASTÉLLI

Kastélli (sometimes known as Kastélli Kissámou) is a bustling and prosperous town serving the local agricultural community. Here you are likely to come across furniture makers at work outside their workshops, cobblers making Cretan riding boots, and old-fashioned bakers using wood-fired ovens. The museum in the main square has long been closed for restoration. If it ever re-opens it is worth visiting for its fine collection of Roman statuary, including finds from Diktýnna, the 2nd-century AD temple that sits at the tip of the Rodopós peninsula, to the east of Kastélli. A rough track leads across the peninsula to the temple site but it is not recommended for cars. Instead, it is better to hire a boat from nearby Kolymvári (*see p108*).

Kastélli is 43km (27 miles) west of Chaniá.

KASTÉLLI ENVIRONS
Polirínia

Some 7km (4 miles) south of Kastélli is the ancient city of Polirínia, a rare example of the kind of city that developed in the post-Minoan era. Cretan society ceased to be highly centralised, and scores, if not hundreds, of small communities were set up, each controlling their own territory. It was probably the lack of water that resulted in Polirínia's abandonment, though the inhabitants did not move far – only down to the base of the hill to the site of today's village, where springs are abundant. From this village, several paths lead uphill to the church (usually locked), built on the site of a Hellenistic-era temple and incorporating Roman masonry into its external walls. From the church, a broad path leads through flower-filled olive groves to the massive walls that surrounded the ancient city. Higher still are the jumbled ruins of fortifications built when the site was briefly reoccupied in the 10th to 13th centuries. Winding through the walls are goat tracks that eventually lead to the crest of the hill, from where there are fine views over the Gulf of Kíssamos (Kólpos Kissámou).

Falásarna

The ancient port city of Falásarna lies to the west of Kastélli, and is well worth visiting both for its ruins and for the huge and little-visited sandy beach. Approaching Falásarna from Plátanos, there are fine views down onto the beach and across the Gramvoúsa peninsula. The port ruins are some 1.5km (1 mile) from the Falásarna

Hotel, near the end of a rough track. Passing masses of polythene tunnels, you know you have nearly reached the site when you pass a large and prominent stone 'throne' on the left (its real purpose is not known). The site is littered with equally huge blocks of tufa that have tumbled from the ancient city's collapsed walls over the years.

The entrance is located next to a prominent circular tower, also part of the city's 3rd-century BC defences, alongside of which is a square cistern with its original plaster-and-pitch lining intact. From here you descend to the flat harbour basin, once under water, but now left high and dry by tectonic movements that have lifted this western end of Crete by about 9m (30ft). Square trenches in the base of the harbour have been left open by archaeologists, at the bottom of which you can see massive masonry blocks jumbled up with pebbles. The theory is that the harbour, built in the 4th century BC, had virtually fallen out of use by the 1st century, but, being enclosed and hidden, was used by pirates as a base for attacking Roman ships. Once the Romans had conquered Crete, they therefore deliberately and permanently blocked the harbour entrance with these huge stones.

If you have the energy, you can climb the hill to the northwest of the harbour, passing little Ágios Gíorgios church, to reach the hilltop acropolis, with its fine views. Alternatively, you can simply enjoy swimming from the nearby beach and exploring the many rock pools.

Falásarna: a beautiful golden beach at the western end of Crete

Wildflowers abound in and around the spectacular Arádena Gorge

CHÓRA SFAKION

Off-season Chóra Sfakion is a quiet, unspoiled fishing village on the south coast which makes the ideal base for a hideaway holiday if all you want to do is walk, swim and enjoy good food in waterside tavernas. However, from May to October it is also the bustling transit point for swarms of hungry hikers coming off ferries from Agía Rouméli, the exit of the Samaria Gorge, to take buses back to Chaniá. The ferry service also links Chóra Sfakion with Soúgia, Palaióchora and Gávdos island (for all of which, *see pp120–21*). The timetable changes regularly, so be sure to check when and where the boat actually calls! *75km (47 miles) southeast of Chaniá.*

West of Chóra Sfakion

Only one road goes west of Chóra Sfakion, a twisting, steep and narrow road that drops vertiginously away to the south and is not recommended to nervous drivers. This passes, just to the west of the town, a group of beachside caves. One of these is named the Cave of Daskaloyiánnis in honour of the 18th-century rebel who led the Cretan struggle against Turkish rule and reputedly used the cave as a hideout. Daskaloyiánnis came from Anópoli, the next village along the road, once a rebel stronghold, now renowned for its carpets of spring wildflowers. Here there is a choice of routes: on foot to Loutró, or by car, along a newly made road, to Arádena. The delightful village of Loutró, about two hours' walk due south along a steep downhill footpath, is the site of an ancient harbour, to which St Paul was heading when his boat was blown off course. (He was eventually shipwrecked off Malta.) It sits on a very beautiful bay, with the added attraction that the only way in and out is by boat or on foot – though this has not deterred recent villa development.

Arádena, by contrast, is a near-deserted village and a delight to explore. It sits on a stony arid plateau, backed by the Lefká Órí (White Mountains) whose peaks rise sheer behind. Like several other isolated and abandoned villages on Crete, the former inhabitants migrated to other parts of the island – or even overseas – in order to make a better living. Some have returned and are starting to restore the decayed buildings, and one wealthy family has donated the new iron bridge that provides access to the village across the spectacular Arádena Gorge. Hand-painted signs in the village point down deserted cobbled streets to the white-domed church of Mikhaíl Archángelos, with its 14th-century frescoes, just visible through the door-grille if the church is locked. To the right of the church is the old road, a broad pebbled path that was the only way into and out of the village until the new bridge was built. The path leads to the edge of the ravine and then plunges down into it, following a zigzag path up the other side. If you follow this path (well worth doing for views and the wildflowers) allow about an hour to reach the top on the other side.

East of Chóra Sfakion

East of Chóra Sfakion the countryside is flat and intensively cultivated, with a rash of villa developments. The only historic site of note is the atmospheric Fragkokástelo, a Venetian fortress that looks remarkably complete from a distance, though only the external walls survive to any height. The castle was built in 1371, ostensibly to protect the southern coast against piratical raids. In fact the castle was more often used for quelling the local population. Nearly 400 men lost their lives in this peaceful spot in 1828 when Cretan insurrectionists, led by Khátzi Mikhális Daliánis, were massacred by an overwhelming force of Turkish soldiers. Local people say that a ghostly army, known as the *drossoulítes* (literally 'dew shades'), returns at dawn to dance on the plain in front of the castle on the anniversary of the massacre, 17 May. Despite a grim history, the castle is tailor-made for children to explore and stands beside a fine and sandy beach, washed by warm and shallow waters.

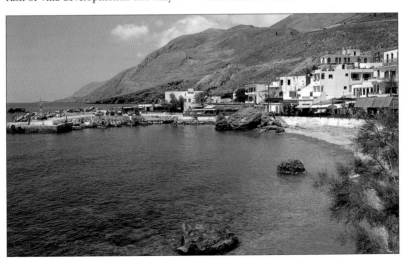

Once a sleepy fishing village, Chóra Sfakion now has a choice of hotels

Moní Goniás is situated right by the sea

KOLYMVÁRI

Much of the coastline west of Chaniá has been developed for tourism, and only when you get as far as Kolymvári do you return to the real Crete. Local people come here for the renowned seafood restaurants, but few tourists follow in their wake. Those who do will find an attractive and self-confident town with a pebble beach, numerous rock pools and crystal-clear waters teeming with small fish.

The Diktýnna

Boat operators offer trips from Kolymvári out to the northeastern tip of the Rodopós peninsula, site of the Diktýnna, one of the ancient world's most famous temples. The Diktýnna or Diktiynnaion thrived from Hellenistic times (the 3rd century BC) through to the Roman era. The goddess Díktynna was, like Diana, a huntress, usually depicted with her dogs, protectress of the mountains and countryside. She was worshipped all over the Greek, and subsequently the Roman, world, with temples to her honour in Marseille, Athens and Sparta. This was her chief sanctuary and it has been suggested that Díktynna represents the survival of a deity from Minoan times – she may have derived from the mountain mother goddess worshipped in Minoan peak sanctuaries. This temple was visible from far out at sea, but the remains, excavated in 1942 by occupying German troops, now consist of little more than a massive paved terrace on which her shrine once stood. The lack of visible structures does not deter visitors from coming here, however, because the sheltered cove below the sanctuary site is excellent for swimming.

Ágios Ioánnis Church

An even less accessible site on the peninsula is the church of Ágios Ioánnis (St John), reached by means of a very rough track (the walk takes two to three hours) from Rodopós. This is the route taken by thousands of pilgrims every year on 29 August (the feast of the birth of St John the Baptist), when boys sharing the name John (Ioánnis) are brought from all over the island for mass baptism. For the rest of the year this lonely shrine is deserted.

Goniás Monastery

Much closer to Kolymvári is the lovely Moní Goniás which dates mainly from its rebuilding in 1662, though it incorporates masonry of several periods. An early 17th-century stone balcony to the right of the gatehouse is supported on brackets carved with ferocious Venetian lions. Opposite the gatehouse is a Turkish fountain (1708), whose inscription reads: 'O flowing spring, pour water for me; water is vital to life, the sweetest element'. Through the gatehouse is the graceful monastic church containing fine examples of woodcarving, such as the abbot's chair.

Best of all are the outstanding 17th-century icons: those on the iconostasis of the central nave are the work of a Cretan monk called Parthenios. An icon in the north aisle (dated 1637 and signed by Konstantinou Paleokaia, also known as Palaiókapas) shows St Nicholas in bishop's robes seated on a scarlet cushion. Adjacent is an earlier work, the mid-15th-century figure of Christ as High Priest. The serene Virgin and Child in the south aisle is of the mid-17th-century period.

To the east of the church is a shady terrace with views to the distant hills of the Akrotíri peninsula. Embedded in the rear wall of the church is a cannon ball from the Turkish bombardment of 1866, when the monastery came under attack for its role in the rebellion against Turkish rule. To the left of the church is a small museum with an outstanding icon, *The Crucifixion* (1637) by Palaiókapas.

Goniás monastery is 1km (⅔ mile) north of Kolymvári.
Closed 12.30–4pm & all day Sat.

The picturesque village of Kolymvári that has so far escaped development

German war graves at Máleme

MÁLEME

The German invasion of Crete began at Máleme on 20 May 1941 (see p112), and today, it is the site of the German War Cemetery. The cemetery stands on Hill 107 where much of the fighting took place and where many of the German paratroopers who took part in the airborne invasion were picked off with bullets as they floated to the ground. The statistics of the battle make grim reading and are a sober reminder that more than three times as many Germans died in the campaign as did Commonwealth troops (6,580 German troops killed or missing, compared with 2,000 on the Commonwealth side). The small pavilion at the entrance to the cemetery, with its map showing the progress of the battle, does not record how many Cretans suffered in this war – for it was they who bore the brunt of the awful reprisals taken by the Germans once the island was in their hands.

Today Hill 107 is a peaceful spot; the lower part is managed to encourage wildflowers in spring, and the upper part is packed with neat graves that spread all the way up to the hill crest. Here a terrace offers views over Máleme airstrip, the focus of the German assault and still in military use today. *Máleme is 16km (10 miles) west of Chaniá.*

MÁLEME ENVIRONS
Spiliá

The countryside south of Máleme is dotted with small village churches that are far older than a first glance would suggest. Three in particular are worth a visit. Spiliá is reached by heading west to the Kolymvári crossroads, then south for 3km (2 miles). Drive on through the village of Spiliá until you see a blue signpost pointing right to the church at the village exit. You first pass a little square on the right, shaded with plane trees and with a little gabled fountain in one corner. The church is another 500m (1,640ft) on from the square, on a grassy mound to the right of a sharp bend. The simple building dates from the 12th century and the soot-blackened frescoes inside from the 14th century. They depict scenes from the Life of the Virgin, including a lively Nativity with the Three Kings on the south wall, and the Presentation of Jesus in the Temple on the opposite wall.

Ágios Stéphanos

From Spiliá drive on south through Drakóna, then, after 1.5km (1 mile), look for a white sign pointing right to Ágios Stéphanos church. This 10th-century building lies at the end of an oak-shaded path renowned for the white cyclamen that flower on the left-hand bank in spring (these cyclamen – *Cyclamen creticum* – are similar to *Cyclamen repandum* found on mainland Greece).

The walls of the ancient church are cracked and subsiding, but the 13th-century frescoes remain clear enough for a Nativity scene to be made out, and, below it, the Stoning of St Stephen, the first Christian martyr, while next to both is a Pentecostal scene. Evangelists are painted round the tiny apse, but the scenes on the south wall are far more difficult to interpret.

Mikhaíl Archángelos

Just 1km (⅔ mile) further south a big sign points right to the extraordinary church of Mikhaíl Archángelos, known as the Rotonda because of its unusual central dome. From the outside this consists of a stepped series of concentric rings, diminishing in size as they climb upwards. Inside, the church resembles a beehive, with the side walls pierced by six tall arches, one of which frames the apse. On the floor there are the remains of 6th-century mosaics with a geometric pattern, while frescoes of standing saints cover several walls.

The church is unique in its plan and shape, and archaeological excavations are in progress in and around the church, aimed at discovering more about its history. These suggest that the church is a rare survivor of the so-called First Byzantine period (mid-5th to mid-6th century), but with frescoes from the 10th and 12th centuries.

Cyclamen

Cyclamen creticum, found nowhere else in the world other than Crete, favours the island's shady gorges and scrubby woodland. Considerably smaller and less showy than its cultivated relatives, its delicate white flowers and leaves appear between March and May with the plant surviving and spreading underground by tubers outside this period.

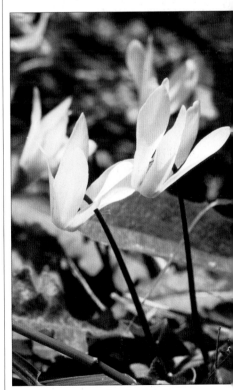

The *Cyclamen creticum*: found only in Crete

The Battle of Crete

The Battle of Crete took place in May 1941, but the events remain a talking point in the island's cafés to this very day, and carefully tended war memorials are found on the main squares of almost every village on the island. These record the names of men, women and children, priests and abbots, shot in reprisal for Cretan acts of resistance during the war.

Churchill's plan

Churchill intended that Crete should be a safe haven for Allied troops driven south through Greece by the seemingly inexorable progress of German troops during the spring of 1941. He referred to Crete as an island fortress, believing that the British Mediterranean Fleet would be able to keep the Germans at bay, whilst the 32,000 British, Greek, Australian and New Zealand troops evacuated from Greece and the Balkans recouped their strength.

For a while this plan succeeded, and the Allied fleet drove off several attempts by German ships to invade the island. Frustrated, the Germans threw tens of thousands of troops into an airborne attack on Crete, which began on 20 May 1941. Parachutists rained out of the sky over the Máleme airstrip (*see p110*). Many were shot before they even touched down and others were killed by Cretan villagers, armed with primitive clubs and pitchforks, as they struggled to release themselves from

their parachutes. For several hours the Allied troops beat off the attack, but, at a critical moment, poor communications led to Hill 107 being evacuated, and the Germans seized the advantage. With this hill secured, it was not long before German troop planes were landing at Máleme without resistance.

The evacuation

Realising that all was lost, Allied commanders concentrated on evacuating their weary troops from Crete as fast as possible. This involved an arduous trek through the White Mountains to the southern shores of Crete where, under heavy aerial bombardment, ships took the troops off to the Egyptian port of Alexandria. It would have been a simple matter for the Germans to have halted this evacuation, if they had not been held up by an heroic regiment of Greek troops who defended a strategic river crossing for two whole days.

The aftermath

German reprisals against the Cretan population for the troops lost in the invasion only served to increase resistance. Local people kept up relentless guerrilla warfare against the invaders – at a heavy cost in terms of human life – for the entire duration of the war.

An exhibit at the Maritime Museum of Crete

MONÍ ARKADÍOU

A symbol of Cretan heroism in the cause of independence and a literal expression of the Cretan battle cry: 'Freedom or Death', Moní Arkadíou has now been designated a European Memorial of Freedom. It was here that hundreds of resistance fighters blew themselves up rather than surrender to the Turks during the 1866–9 revolt. Huge numbers of people converge on the monastery every 9 November to commemorate the anniversary of the mass suicide.

The siege and its aftermath

The siege began on 7 November 1866, when Turkish soldiers surrounded the monastery. Hundreds of Cretan guerrillas had sought refuge inside, along with their wives and children. The Turks eventually demolished the now-rebuilt gatehouse, and poured into the deserted monastery courtyard.

Abbot Gabriel instructed the Cretan defenders to withdraw to the now-roofless gunpowder store, which is at the far left-hand side of the courtyard. He waited until the last minute before giving the word to light the powder kegs, so as to trap and kill as many Turks as possible in the explosion. The abbot was killed by the Turks, and a rebel called Kostis Giamboudakis blew up the kegs.

Nearly 300 rebels were killed, as were 600 women and children, along with 1,500 Turks. Only 34 Greeks escaped, and another 100 were taken into captivity and tortured.

The event stirred complacent politicians into action all around Europe. Until then, powerful countries – Britain, France and Italy included – had stood by idly and ignored the atrocities being committed by the Turks in Crete. It took another 30 years for Crete to gain a semblance of self-determination.

Museum memorial

In the centre of the courtyard is the church with its fine baroque façade (dated 1587). To the right, the museum is full of mementoes of the siege: Turkish swords and cannon, portraits of some of those who died, the vestments of Abbot Gabriel and, most poignant of all, the shrapnel-scarred and hand-painted banner of the Cretans who died in the defence of the monastery.
Moní Arkadíou is 26km (16 miles) southeast of Réthymno. Museum open: daily 8am–7pm.

MONÍ ARKADÍOU ENVIRONS
Eléfterna

Eléfterna is the site of a fascinating post-Minoan hilltop town. Just beyond the village entrance sign, a concrete track leads downhill to the right, signposted 'To Ancientry' (*sic*). This leads to a Roman villa built of materials salvaged from ancient Eléfterna – the sheer quantity of richly carved marble indicates the wealth of that city.

Heading back up the idyllic gorge, you will pass a fine 10th-century church beside a spring. Back in the village turn right and follow signs to the Acropolis Taverna. Parking by the taverna, you can follow the track to the right that leads to the ancient hilltop city, poised on a ridge between two deep gorges.

The most prominent of the ruins is a late-Roman tower; note how the rock-cut path in front of it has been carved into a grid to resemble paving. A rock-cut path goes to the left of the tower and after some 300m (980ft) runs out – turn left here and, immediately on the left, you will find a series of huge rock-cut cisterns, of cathedral-like proportions, cut into the cliffs below the city, and supported by a forest of pillars.

65km (40 miles) to the east of Réthymno by road (10km/6 miles by footpath).

Moní Arkadíou church, with its baroque façade, has become a symbol of Cretan heroism

MONÍ PRÉVELI

Moní Préveli enjoys an idyllic setting on the steep hills that sweep down to the sea on the south of the island. One 19th-century traveller described the setting as a Cretan paradise, and 'one of the most happily chosen spots for a retreat from the cares and responsibilities of life'. In fact, Moní Préveli has seen more than its share of tumultuous events and is another of those monasteries that have played a conspicuous role in Cretan history.

Centre of resistance

The monastery was founded in the 16th century, on a site that lies further inland: the ruins of the original monastery still stand, alongside the Megapótamos River, on the road up to the present-day monastery. It was moved to this more secluded position after the Turks took Crete. The new monastery, with its precious library, became a clandestine centre of learning under the Turkish occupation, and successive abbots took a leading role in organising local revolts against the Turks.

From 1866 on, following the explosion that killed the rebels at Moní Arkadíou (*see p114*), British sympathisers with the Cretan cause raised funds to buy a ship – the *Arkhadi*. This made regular trips to Crete, through the Turkish blockade, carrying weapons and supplies for the Cretan rebels, which were landed at the beach just to the east of this spot; again it was the monks of Moní Préveli who organised their distribution.

The battle of Crete

Moní Préveli also played a key role in sheltering Commonwealth troops during the evacuation that took place at the end of the Battle of Crete in May 1941 (*see p112*). The same beach below the monastery was used by the

The seemingly isolated Préveli monastery has often been at the centre of momentous events

The Megapótamos River joins the sea at Préveli

submarines that took troops off the island to the Egyptian port of Alexandria. A plaque in the monastery courtyard records the fact that hundreds of British, Australian and New Zealand soldiers were protected by the monks and guided to the beachhead from where they made their escape, all this 'in defiance of the ferocious reprisals suffered by the monks'.

The monastery today

Amongst the reprisals taken by the Germans was the partial destruction of the monastic complex. The monks themselves, however, had already destroyed what ancient building fabric and frescoes had remained from the 17th century in their own rebuilding works in 1835. The buildings today are therefore relatively recent, but they make a harmonious ensemble.

The church contains a splendidly carved and gilded iconostasis, covered in scenes from the Life of Christ. Some of these date from the mid-18th century, and have been transferred here from

churches in the Préveli region to protect them from theft. The monastic museum is housed in the former stables where rock-cut mangers are now used as display cabinets. Exhibits include liturgical silver, and the vestments (dated 1701–10) of Abbot Jacob Préveli, the monastery's founder.

Monastery open: summer, daily 9am–7pm; winter, 9am–5pm. Museum closed: 1–3pm. Admission charge.

Palm Beach

The little beach, which has so often featured in the history of Moní Préveli and Crete, lies to the east of the monastery, and can be reached from the monastic complex along a marked path. Allow at least half an hour and be prepared for some scrambling over steep and rocky terrain (for an alternative route *see p143*). If the beach is not too crowded, this can be a lovely spot.

The Megapótamos River flows into the sea at this point, and its banks are lined by groves of beautiful palm trees, the same rare Cretan native palms that grow at Vái (*see p71*). The whole estuary resembles a desert oasis, backed by the harsh rocks of the Kourtaliotiko ravine. From the beach, you can continue eastwards, along rough tracks, for another 3km (2 miles) to the church of Agía Fotinis, one of numerous little churches lining this part of the southern coast. Agía Fotinis dates from the late 14th century, and its walls feature frescoes of the female saints, Fotiní, Marína, Paraskeví, Kyriakí and Eiríni.

Moní Préveli is 38km (24 miles) south of Réthymno (see p142 for a suggested route).

Priests and monks

If your idea of a typical priest or monk is that of a humble, pious and charitable person, think again when it comes to Crete. Monks, especially, and many priests regard themselves as the aristocrats of the island and it is not unusual for them to treat those they consider their inferiors with a degree of arrogance that is quite untypical of Crete as a whole.

Focus of learning and resistance

Cretans know the score and pretend a head-bowing deference to any monk that crosses their path. This exaggerated respect, afforded even by the most cynical of atheists, can be attributed to the key role played by the Greek Orthodox Church during the dark years of the Turkish occupation, and again during the German occupation when the Church served as the focal point for Cretan resistance. Priests and monks also ran clandestine schools under Turkish rule, in defiance of the ban on Christian education and worship, keeping alive the flame of Greek nationalism. Great acts of heroism were committed by the predecessors of today's monks and priests. The major powers ignored the plight of Crete under the Turks until the rebels of Arkadíou monastery (see p114) committed mass suicide in 1866. This event drew attention to Turkish brutality, galvanising Europe into belated action. Again, during World

War II, the monks at Préveli monastery (see p116) suffered vicious reprisals because of the help they gave to Allied troops escaping the island by submarine to Egypt.

Waning influence

For all this, memories of the past are beginning to fade and the influence of the Church in the everyday life of the Cretan people is on the wane, at least in the urban centres. Even so, monks (who remain chaste) and priests (who are allowed to marry) maintain a highly visible presence in Cretan society, with their uncut locks and beards and their black cassocks, and no Cretan would consider an event in the life of the community complete – whether a school prize-giving or a wine festival – without the blessing and official presence of the clergy.

Monks and priests are a highly visible and integral part of life on the Island

Palaióchora is also known as the 'Sunland'

PALAIÓCHORA

From being a small southern coast fishing village, Palaióchora has recently expanded to become one of the island's most enjoyable upmarket resorts. Several new – but small – hotels have been built, and new restaurants have sprung up along with them, although without spoiling the Cretan character. That Cretan character extends to the fact that the town centre is virtually sealed off to traffic at night, when local people leave their houses to play backgammon and drink *raki* outside the local tavernas, their chairs and tables filling the narrow streets.

Palaióchora has two big beaches that can both be viewed from the castle that sits high above the town, built in 1279 by the Venetians and consisting now of little but the encircling walls. To the left (east) of the town is the ferry harbour and then a huge sweep of mixed sand and shingle beach. To the right (west) is a huge beach of golden sand – flying its European Blue Flag (awarded to beaches that meet the highest standards of cleanliness) with pride. The waters on this side can be cold because of the mountain streams that pour into the bay to the west. In the height of summer this is welcome, but earlier in the year it deters all but the very hardiest of swimmers.

Offshore breezes make this a good spot for windsurfing too, and there is a hut at the far northwestern end of the beach where boards are available for hire.

South coast ferries

If you want a break from baking in the sun all day, you can take the south coast ferry from Palaióchora's harbour and head along the coast, or across the sea to the island of Gávdos. Tickets and timetables are available from travel agents in the town, or from the ferry company kiosk on the harbour.

The ferries operate between the beginning of April and the end of

October. During this period there are daily services to the Elafonísi islands, to the west of Palaióchora (*see p138*), and eastwards to Soúgia (*see below*) and Ayía Rouméli (for the Samaria Gorge). Services operate five times a week in summer from Palaióchora, three times a week from Chóra Sfakíon. Off-season the service is limited.

For information, tel: (28230) 41393.

Palaióchora is 84km (52 miles) southwest of Chaniá.

PALAIÓCHORA ENVIRONS
Soúgia

Remotely located at the end of a long, twisting road from Chaniá, Soúgia is gradually being discovered by tourists for its pebbly beach, translucent waters and simple fish tavernas lining the shore. Across the sea lies the distant island of Gávdos, while across the beach, to the east, you can make out the remains of the ancient Roman port of Elyros either side of a small river estuary. To the west

of the village, a well-marked path (very steep in places) makes for the ruins of a 4th-century BC temple to Asklepios (god of healing) at Lissós, some 3km (2 miles) across the cliffs.

Gávdos

Gávdos island is worth a trip if you want to say that you have stood on the most southerly point in Europe. The island is about two hours south of Crete by ferry, and the day-trip allows you four hours to explore the tiny harbour at Karabé or walk inland to the main village of Kastrí (where there is precious little to see). Most of the islanders are farmers eking a living from the sunbleached soil. The landscape is flat and unremarkable, but there are some fine beaches and the turquoise waters are delightful for bathing. Local people have taken to meeting the ferry and providing transport to the island's best beaches, which lie to the north, or to the southernmost tip of the island, and of Europe, Tripití point.

Palaióchora's Venetian castle walls rise above the ferry harbour

Réthymno

Réthymno is a very likeable town from which vehicles have largely been excluded, leaving the narrow streets to the bustling hubbub of human traffic. Watching the parade of people up and down the main street is an enthralling pastime, especially from the comfort of one of the numerous pavement cafés clustering round the Rimóndi Fountain. The shopping is excellent (if more expensive than Chaniá) and the town remains essentially Cretan, with traditional boot-makers, and ironmongers selling axes and sickles, mixed in amongst the tourist shops selling embroidery, lace and T-shirts.

A view of Réthymno at night

Another feature of the city is its architecture, a legacy of Venetian and Turkish rule. Look up in almost any street and you are sure to see ornamental balconies and elaborate window frames above the modern

Réthymno's café-lined Venetian Harbour is the centre of the city's bustling nightlife

Réthymno town plan (*see pp134–5 for walk*)

shopfronts. Look down alleys and you will see doorways carved with coats of arms, cherubs, vines or crouching lions, or crumbling façades propped up by timber buttresses waiting to be restored.

Archaeological Museum

Réthymno's Archaeological Museum is housed within one of the defensive bastions opposite the main gate of the Venetian Fort (*see p125*). Light floods into the museum from its central atrium, around which are top-quality displays of sculpture, funerary chests, coins, pottery and jewellery from excavations in Réthymno province.

The museum provides an excellent introduction to all the various crafts

practised by the Minoans. Here you will find beautiful and delicate pottery that would not look out of place on a modern dinner table. From various caves and peak sanctuaries in the province there are clay figures of priestesses and bulls. There is also a large display of clay *larnakes* (burial chests) painted with abstract renderings of sea creatures, such as octopuses, fish and nautilus shells. Others depict lively hunting scenes, suggesting that the Minoan countryside was alive with deer, wild horned goats and flowers.

The dead were placed in these *larnakes*, trussed up tight in the foetal position, knees to chin, and the chests were then placed in chambered tombs.

Beneath the walls of the Fortétza

Some *larnakes* have a hole in the base, which has led some archaeologists to suggest that they may originally have been used as domestic bathtubs. Such an explanation seems a touch far-fetched, as do the tortuous attempts of Minoan archaeologists to prove that the sacred double axe symbol – the *labrys* – bears a geometrical relationship to the form of the labyrinth,

the maze-like pattern that appears on coinage of the period from the 6th century BC. Examples of both coins and axes are displayed here.

Finally there is an unusually good display of Graeco-Roman statuary, including a very fine bronze helmeted youth (probably Mercury) salvaged from a Roman ship wrecked off Agía Galíni on the south coast.

VENETIAN RULE

The Venetians changed the face of Réthymno and the whole of Crete during the 465 years of their rule (1204–1669). Venice acquired the island by questionable means (as part of the spoils of the Fourth Crusade) but compensated by building harbours, shipyards, fortresses, palaces and public buildings. At first, Venetian rule was exploitative; timber was stripped from the hillsides, heavy taxes imposed, and Catholicism was forced on the Cretan people, whipping up resentment amongst the Orthodox clergy. In time, however, a more fruitful relationship evolved, with Cretans and Venetians intermarrying and sending their children to Italy to be educated. As a result, the arts flourished in the 16th and 17th centuries, the period known as the Cretan Renaissance. This was the era that produced Mikhaíl Damaskinós, the great icon painter (see p38), and the even more famous El Greco (see p36).

*Opposite the main entrance to the
Venetian Fortress. Tel: (28310) 54668.
Open: Tue–Sun 8am–5pm.
Closed: Mon. Admission charge.*

Historical and Folk Art Museum

Now housed in a fine 17th-century
Venetian mansion close to the
Nerantzies Mosque, this is a charming
collection of traditional Cretan crafts:
embroidery, lace, basketware, farming
tools, costumes and pottery.
*Odós Vernadóu 28–30.
Open: Mon–Sat 9am–2pm & 6–8pm.
Admission charge.*

Venetian Fortress
(also known as the Fortétza)

Réthymno's massive fortress dominates
distant views of the town and seems big
enough to accommodate the whole
population of Réthymno in times of
trouble. It is said to be the biggest
Venetian fortress ever built and the
impressive walls encompass churches, an
open-air theatre, and a whole network
of underground magazines and cisterns,
as well as ruined accommodation blocks
for garrison troops. A climb through the
pine-planted interior is worthwhile just
for the views, especially at sunset.

An elegant minaret, a legacy of Turkish rule, points skyward from Réthymno's close-packed city centre

Spectacular scenery surrounds walkers in the Samaria Gorge

Alternatively, you can watch day turn to night from the Sunset taverna, which sits on the coastal road, below the west-facing fortress walls.

The marvellous views emphasise the strategic value of this particular headland, and its fortress was built in 1573, specifically as a base from which to stamp out piracy. In this it succeeded, but the fortress did not prove much of a defence when the Turks arrived in 1645, seizing the city after a siege of only 23 days – a trifle compared with Iraklíon's 21-year standoff. The Turks built the big domed mosque, the most prominent building in the interior.

Odós Salaminos. Open: daily in summer 8.30am–7pm (6pm in winter). Admission charge.

Samaria Gorge (Farangi Samariás)

After Knossós, the Samaria Gorge is the best-known attraction on Crete, and every summer tens of thousands of people trudge the 15-km (9-mile) long path that follows the bottom of the gorge, finding none of the tranquillity and solitude that one normally associates with walking in the countryside. If you hate crowds, set out early in the day (the gorge opens at 6am) or walk one of Crete's other, equally spectacular, ravines.

The gorge is only open from the beginning of May to the end of October because flash floods are a very real danger in the rainy season.

There is no road access to the southern end, so your only way back is by ferry (to Chóra Sfakíon, Soúgia or Palaióchora), or by retracing your steps up the gorge (there are rooms to rent in Agía Rouméli, at the southern end of the gorge, so it is perfectly feasible to do this over two days).

The times of ferries and connecting buses can be checked at one of Crete's tourist information centres (the times vary according to the season). Of course, you can leave the logistics of getting to and from the gorge to somebody else by signing up for a coach excursion, though this means setting out with a crowd of 30 or more people. You can also hire a taxi to get you there and arrange to be collected at Agía Rouméli. One or two taxis are available for hire in Agía Rouméli itself, and they will take you back to Chaniá or anywhere else on the island – provided you get to them before someone else does. If all else fails, there are plenty of rooms for rent in Soúgia, Palaióchora and Chóra Sfakíon, where you can spend the night.

In the gorge

The total length of the gorge is 13km (8 miles), and it is another 2km (1¼ miles) to the coastal village of Agía Rouméli with kilometre posts marking out the route. You should allow at least five hours to do the walk. Keep your entrance ticket as you will be asked to hand it in at the exit – this is a simple device to help the park wardens count the number of people in the gorge, and send in the rescue services, if necessary, to locate stranded walkers. You should take sufficient food and drink to sustain you along the route (there are tavernas at either end, but not within the gorge itself). Drinking water is supplied from taps at six points along the gorge, four of which also have toilets.

The lazy way

If you do not feel like tackling the whole gorge, there are two alternatives. One is to walk the first 2km (1¼ miles) or so from the northern end of the gorge; this is exhilarating, because the route plunges some 900m (2,953ft) down the so-called Xylóskalo ('Wooden Staircase'), through beautiful pine woods; the obvious drawback is that you have to climb all the way back up, and 900m (2,953ft) of staircase is no joke.

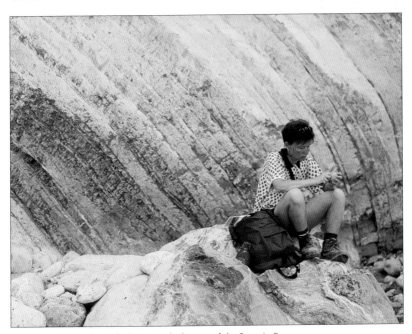

Pausing for thought and refreshment at the bottom of the Samaria Gorge

The other option, known as 'The Lazy Route', is to tackle the gorge from the southern end. Despite the name, this involves a stiff uphill climb to the gorge entrance (2km/1¼ miles), followed by a walk of about 4km (2½ miles) through the narrowest part of the gorge, where the path is squeezed between towering cliffs, up to 600m (1,969ft) high. You can go all the way up to the gorge's most famous landmark, the so-called Iron Gates (Sidherespórtes), where the sides of the gorge close in to leave a gap of a mere 3m (10ft). To get here involves a there-and-back walk of about 11km (7 miles), so you might just as well walk the whole gorge.

The Samaria Gorge begins 43km (27 miles) south of Chaniá, on the Omalós Plateau, and runs southwards to end 2km (1¼ miles) north of Agía Rouméli. Admission charge, and boat fare to Chóra Sfakion.

THE VÁMOS PENINSULA

The Vámos peninsula east of Chaniá has recently been 'discovered' by upmarket tour operators, so that its coastal villages – Kalýves, Almrída and Georgioúpoli – are developing a rash of new villa complexes around their margins. For the present, they remain largely unspoiled, and make an excellent base from which to explore western Crete by car.

Despite the crowds, nothing detracts from the adventure of walking the gorge

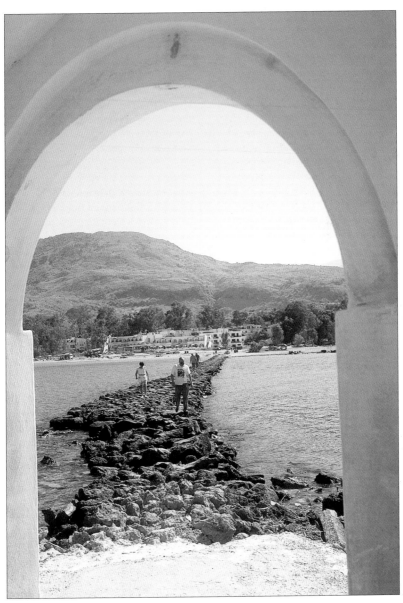

Georgioúpoli is one of several upmarket resorts on the Vámos peninsula

Georgioúpoli

Georgioúpoli is named after Prince George, son of the King of Greece, who was appointed High Commissioner of Crete from 1898 to 1906, ruling the island in the interim period when Crete still technically belonged to Turkey, but enjoyed a measure of autonomy. The prince used to enjoy coming here for the hunting, and the area is still renowned for its bird life. The Almirós River flows into the sea at this point, and the marshy margins of the river are a haven for birds, as well as for freshwater crabs, terrapins, frogs and fish. Locally the Almirós is known as the 'Turtle River', and you can hire pedal boats or take boat trips at the village's fishing harbour for exploring its reed-fringed banks.

Georgioúpoli also sits on the western edge of a huge and often deserted sandy beach that spreads for 12km (7 miles) in the direction of Réthymno.

Vrýses and Samonás

Another attractive feature of Georgioúpoli is the wonderful green avenue of giant eucalyptus trees that forms the old road out of the village (once the main road, but now superseded by the National Highway). Following this will bring you to pretty Vrýses, famous for its creamy yoghurt and wild honey, and on to Néo Chorió. Here it is well worth diverting to Samonás for Crete's most appealingly sited church, Ágios Nikólaos. If you want to go inside the church, call at the house of the guardian, which is on the left at the village exit. The guardian or his wife will come with you and open up the church.

Just beyond the village you will catch your first glimpse of the church, beautifully sited on a knoll in a lovely green valley, with no other building in sight. Built of attractive honey-coloured stone, with a tall central dome, the church dates from the 11th century, and the frescoes inside, including a tender Virgin and Child, were made sometime between 1230–36.

Áptera

After the detour to Samonás, the road through Stílos passes a turning, just before Megála Khoráfia, that leads to the ruined hilltop city of Áptera. The extent of the overgrown ruins indicates just how large this post-Minoan city was. Its exact foundation date is not known, but it was flourishing in the 7th century BC and was occupied until the Arab conquest of Crete in AD 824. The walls can be traced for a circuit of some 4km (2½ miles), but the most obvious remains are those of the Turkish-era fortress, standing at the highest point on the hill, and offering extensive views over the Vámos peninsula and Soúda Bay. Also visible is a Venetian fort on a prominent hill to the north – this is now used as a prison.

Beaches and wildflowers

Kalýves and Almrída, both on the western edge of the Vámos peninsula, have sandy, gently shelving beaches, perfectly safe for children to play on. Beyond here, a network of narrow lanes threads the peninsula, well worth exploring for the wildflowers.

The northern and eastern edges of the peninsula are stony and exposed to wind, so hundreds of tiny fields have been created by clearing the soil and using the rock to form drystone walls. Stone-paved paths thread their way between the walls, and some fields, no longer cultivated, have been re-colonised by masses of flowers.

If your explorations take you through the village of Gavalochóri, stop to look at the little museum, reached up the lane opposite the war memorial. This contains miscellaneous objects collected by the villagers, from old photographs to weapons from World War II.

Georgioúpoli lies 33km (21 miles) east of Chaniá, 26km (16 miles) west of Réthymno.

The legend of Áptera

The name Áptera means wingless. According to legend this was the site of a competition between the muses and sirens to see who sang better. When the sirens lost, they were so mortified they threw off their wings, which caused them to fall into the sea and drown. Their beautiful white wings were transformed into small islands – identified âs the Lefke Islands in the Soúda Bay.

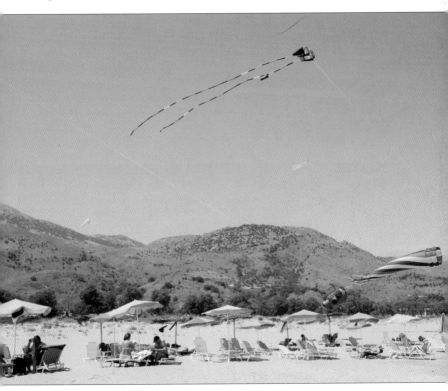

Making the most of the beach at Georgioúpoli

Walk: Chaniá

This walk introduces you to the intricate maze of narrow alleys in the old city and harbour area (*for map of route, see pp98–9*).

Allow 1 hour – but longer if you are tempted to browse in some of Chaniá's best shops.

1 Market hall

Start at the cross-shaped market hall, an elegant neoclassical building of 1911, packed with good things to buy for picnics or presents. From the newspaper kiosk at the centre of the market, head west, past the fish stalls, and exit from the building down the café-lined flight of steps.

Turn right then first left into Odós Skridlóf.

This street is known as 'Leather Alley' for obvious reasons – bags, belts and sandals are hung from the shop awnings in such profusion that it is impossible to proceed at anything other than browsing pace. The prices here are very keen; the only problem is too much choice!

Once through Skridlóf, turn right down Odós Khalídon.

2 Church of Three Martyrs

On the right is the Church of Three Martyrs. Although it has a pleasing façade, this church is disappointingly modern within.

Continue along Odós Khalídon.

You'll find lots of locally-made pottery for sale in Chania

3 Turkish baths

Genuinely ancient, by contrast, are the former Turkish Baths, further down on the right, topped by 12 domes sitting like a dozen eggs in a box. Part of the bathhouse is now used as a bronze-workers' foundry.
Carry on up Odós Khalídon.

4 Archaeological Museum

On the left is the Archaeological Museum, housed in the former Franciscan church (*see p96*), with the stumpy remains of a Gothic campanile (belltower) to the left of the façade.

Beyond the museum is the café-lined Plateía Santriváni, a lively spot at night when buskers and street traders set up their pitch.
Just before the square, turn left into Odós Zambelioú, a typical street in the old city, crammed with characterful shops and old Venetian town houses. Where the street narrows and begins to climb, look for Odós Moschón.

5 Renieri Gate

An alley on the right leads down to the Renieri Gate, with its family coat of arms and inscriptions dating the fine classical gateway to 1608. Through the gate, immediately on the left, is the late 15th-century chapel of the Renieri family, whose town house (now Sultana's restaurant) stands alongside. Ahead, at the end of Odós Moschón, there are several more elegant Venetian palaces, some now converted to up-market hotels.
Turn right beside the medieval-style façade of the Hotel Contessa, then left up steps beside the Amphora Hotel, pausing

In the maze of narrow shop-lined streets of the old Venetian city

at the top to admire the jumble of picturesque alleys that intersect at this photogenic spot. Go straight across, then right down Odós A Gampá.

Another fine Venetian palace (now the Eugenia II Hotel), with ornate stone balconies and window decoration, terminates the street.
Turn right here, down Odós Angeloú, to reach the entrance to the Naval Museum (see p98).

6 Firkás

The museum is set in the restored 16th-century Venetian fortress known as the Firkás. From the walls of the fortress (no charge for entry) there are sweeping views of the whole harbour, with its lighthouse, sea wall, arsenal and domed Mosque of the Janissaries (*see p96*).

To return to the market, follow the harbour back round to Plateía Santriváni, then retrace your steps up Odós Khalídon.

Walk: Réthymno

Réthymno, with its narrow traffic-free streets, tempting shop displays and traditional architecture, is tailor-made for strolling. To make the most of this walk, come at dusk, when the sunset views from the Fortétza are stunning (*for map of route, see p123*).
Allow 1 hour.

Start at the Customs House end of the Venetian Harbour where the fishermen gather to mend their nets. There is a small fish market here most mornings, opposite Benetsianíko's bar, and there is also a good view of the 16th-century Venetian lighthouse.
Turning your back to the harbour, take the road to the left, then second right (Odós Salamínas), then second right (Odós Himárras).

1 Fortétza

This road leads up to the Fortétza, passing first the Centre of Contemporary Art, which hosts temporary exhibitions of modern Greek art. The whole area around the museum is developing as a centre for young artisans, and you can see jewellers, icon painters and potters at work as you stroll. The road ends at the entrance to the **Archaeological Museum**, on the

The Venetian lighthouse

right (*see p123*), and the Fortétza on the left (*see p125*).
Coming out of the Fortétza, head straight down the steep cobbled ramp that leads to Odós Melisinoú, turn left, and then second right (Odós Xanthoúdidou) beside the Fortezza Hotel.

By night this narrow street and all the others in the vicinity are packed with taverna tables. Take the third right (Odós Arambatzogloú), and follow it to the little square at the top. Turn left here (Odós Nikiforoú-Fóka), then first left into Odós Vernadóu.

2 History and Folk Art Museum

This street has many fine houses in the Venetian architectural style, including the grand palazzo, halfway down on the right, which is now the home for the History and Folk Art Museum.
Continue down Odós Vernadóu.

3 Nerantziés Mosque

A short distance further down is the elegant Odeion concert hall, better known as the Nerantziés Mosque. Originally built as a church in the mid-16th century, it was converted to a mosque in 1657 and given its stylish minaret in 1890. Today the building is used as a music school (closed to the public).
At the end of Odós Vernadóu, turn right into the city's crowded main street, Odós Ethníkos Antístáseos. Walk up the street to explore the fascinating range of shops and the market at the far end, up against the 16th-century Porta Guora, all that remains of the Venetian city walls.

Coming back down the street, take the third left (Odós Áyios Fragkískou).

Turkish-style balconies shade the streets

4 Franciscan friary

Take a look at the fine gateway of the 16th-century Franciscan friary, now a school.

5 Rimóndi Fountain

Cafés dominate this end of the street and cluster thickly around the Rimóndi Fountain. Built in 1629, it has three lions' heads spouting water into a marble basin.

6 Loggia

To the right of the fountain, Odós Paleológou contains the 16th-century Loggia, used as a meeting place for the Venetian nobility. This handsome arcaded building has been restored and is now a gallery selling good-quality reproductions of classical art.
From here it is a short step down Odós Nearhoú back to the harbour.

Tour: the Thériso Gorge

This undemanding circular route is an appetiser for more ambitious drives. If you have come to Crete mainly to laze on the beach, consider doing this particular drive, at least, to sample a Byzantine frescoed church and one of Crete's several deep ravines.

Allow 2–3 hours.

From the centre of Chaniá, follow signs for Kastélli. After 3km (2 miles) you will pass a left turn signposted Thériso – ignore this and take the next left turn, at the traffic lights, signposted Omalós. Follow the flat road through orange groves (heady with scent in April and May). After 14km (9 miles) you will reach a major junction with a petrol station at a spot known as **Mnimeio**. Next to this, hidden in a pine grove, is a grim war memorial with a glass altar displaying the skulls of Cretan resistance fighters shot by German firing squads.

Take the right turn (signposted **Alikanós/Soúgia**), crossing over the River Kerítis. On entering Alikanós village turn right, then almost immediately right again, following the signs for Koufós. After 300m (980ft) you will pass **Ágios Yeíryios church**. Take the next right, and continue for 1km (⅔ mile) until you see a red-and-white sign pointing right for **Ágios Cyrgiánnis church**, completely hidden amongst orange groves. This lovely 14th-century church has lost its dome, but this allows light in so that you can study the frescoes of serene saints (painted around 1430), and the two reused 6th-century pillars and capitals to the north of the crossing.

Go back to the petrol station, this time turning right for **Fournés**, passing through more citrus groves with good views of the Lefká Óri (White Mountains) ahead, then climbing gently up a winding river valley dotted with plane trees, oaks and sweet chestnuts. From here, you can start climbing the highest peak of the White Mountains called **Pàchnes** (2,452m/8,045ft).

(Map)

N Ágioi Théodoroi

CHANIÁ

Kastélli

Vamvakopoulos

Soúda

Perivólia

Réthymno

Mourniés

Koufós Ágios
       Cyrgiánnis   Agiá

Mnimeio

Alikanós

Fournés

Spilía

Mesklá

Thériso

Zoúrva

Omalós

N

0   5km

In Fournés, take the left fork to **Mesklá** along a narrow, winding mountain road. On entering Mesklá, find the track on the left, just after the bridge, that leads up to a 14th-century church with well-preserved frescoes in the nave (dated 1303) and in the entrance narthex (mid-15th century).

Carry on up through the village for a short, but adventurous, drive of 11km (7 miles) through **Zoúrva** to **Thériso**. The road, though unmetalled after Zoúrva, is perfectly feasible in a hired car so long as you take it easy.

Thériso, the birthplace of Cretan hero Eleftherias Venizélos, marks the start of the scenic **Thériso Gorge**, whose sheer craggy cliffs tower either side of the road that weaves along the bottom, crossing the river again and again via numerous stone bridges. After 6km (4 miles), the road passes beneath a huge cave set in the base of a cliff, with house-sized boulders strewn about the valley floor. You can stop here to listen to the music of sheep bells echoing across the sides of the gorge and to enjoy the rich and varied wildflowers. Continue on to the end of the gorge, after which it is just 10km (6 miles), on the same road, back to Chaniá.

The Mesklá rebels

Mesklá was the base for a rebellion against Venetian rule in the 16th century. Rebel leader George Kandanoleon ran a rival administration, refusing to pay taxes, until he foolishly sought to make his rule legitimate by marrying his son to the daughter of a Venetian aristocrat. Kandanoleon and his supporters celebrated the marriage in typical Cretan style. When they were all stupefied with food and drink, Venetian troops rounded them all up, and either shot them on the spot, or hanged them in surrounding villages as a grim warning.

Pausing to let the ubiquitous sheep and goats of Crete pass to their grazing grounds

Tour: the Elafonísi islands

Livas, the hot south wind, creates in the islands at the southwestern edge of Crete the largest waves of the Mediterranean Sea. The unspoiled islands and beaches are difficult to reach and this drive once involved covering long distances on winding roads that are sometimes no more than dirt tracks; some of the worst of these have, however, now been resurfaced.

Allow all day.

From **Kastélli Kissámou** take the westward road to Plátanos. Take the right turn to **Falásarna** (*see p104*) to

visit the ruins of the 4th-century BC port. Otherwise continue through this rather dusty and unattractive village on the Sfinári road. The route now passes through scenic hills with the sea always in view. You will glimpse endless rows of plastic tunnels and greenhouses down on the fertile plain below. Growing bananas and out-of-season salad vegetables for export to the Greek mainland is a major industry.

Beyond the villages of **Kámpos** and **Keramotí**, sweeping views open up to the right over Stómio Bay (**Ormos Stómiou**). At Kefáli, turn right immediately after driving through the village, following the sign to **Moní Chrysoskalítissas** ('Golden Stair').

The reason for the name may become apparent once you reach the beautiful white-walled convent with its powder-blue roofs. The convent is set on a sheer-sided rocky outcrop with steps (*skali* in Greek) leading down to a cove. One of the 90 steps is said to be made of gold (*khrisos*), but only those who are free from sin are able to see it! There has been a hermitage here since at least the 13th century. The present buildings were constructed in the mid-19th century and once supported a community of 200 – now reduced to just two.

A new road has replaced the bumps and potholes between Chrysoskalítissas and Elafonísi, and nowadays public buses as well as coach tours make it to the coast. There are also daily boats from Agía Rouméli. Yet despite the crowds this is still Crete's most stunning beach, with its tropical-like, pink-tinged sands, warm clear water, shells, rock pools and darting fish. The sea is shallow enough (less than a metre deep at the maximum) that you can wade to the nearest offshore island to another lovely tree-shaded beach. The resort has a growing number of rooms to rent behind the beach; there is also talk of a new large resort hotel, but on this hotly disputed project the environmentalists may win the day.

Return along the dirt track to Kefáli, turning right to pick up the road to **Élos**. Élos is the capital of the region known as the Kastanochória – the

Wading off the Elafonísi islands

Chestnut Villages – because sweet chestnuts are grown here as a commercial crop (their harvesting is celebrated by a chestnut festival in late October). Come here in July and the air will be thick with the scent of chestnut blossom. In early November the trees turn golden, and in late April the fresh new leaf buds unfurl.

Shortly after **Koutsomatádos**, woodland gives way to the cliffs and caves of the **Topólia Gorge**. After this last burst of excitement, the road descends rapidly to **Kaloudiana**, where you should turn left to return to **Kastélli**, or right to join the Chaniá highway at **Koléni**.

Keramotí village

Tour: the Amári Valley

The Amári Valley is rich in Byzantine churches, providing an excuse to explore an area full of spring wildflowers and little visited by other tourists. The churches are often closed but the key can usually be tracked down quite easily – ask at the nearest *kafeníon*. Take a torch for illuminating the frescoes.

Allow at least half a day.

From Réthymno, follow the Old Road east along the seafront until you come to **Perivólia**, then turn right (signposted Amári) to pass under the National Highway. Shortly afterwards, turn right to Chromonastíri. Just before the village, look for a left turn signposted to **Ágios Efichios**, down a rough 2-km (1¼-mile) long track. The domed church has frescoes dating back to the 12th century – thus making them amongst the earliest to survive on Crete.

Back on the Amári road, continue to **Agía Foteiní**, turning right at the village junction. As you drive through the village, the broad Amári valley is revealed to the left. In Méronas look for the **church of the Panagía** on the left just after the village war memorial. The jumble of frescoes here dates from 1339. The delicate icon of the Virgin is late 14th century, and one of the oldest on Crete.

Backtrack now to Agía Foteiní and turn left immediately after the village exit to **Thrónos**. The tiny church in the village centre, with its Venetian-influenced Gothic portal, has 14th-century frescoes of the Life of the Virgin in the apse and later 15th-century frescoes in the same theme in the nave. Remains of a geometric mosaic continue from the interior to the outside of the church, running up to the excavated footings of its much larger 4th-century predecessor. Further down the street, a concrete path on the left to **Sivrita** (signposted Sybritos) leads uphill to the recently excavated site of the ancient Amári Valley capital, founded around the 5th century BC and still inhabited into the early medieval period.

Return to the main road, and about 2km (1¼ miles) further on (1.5km/ 1 mile beyond the left turn to **Kalóyeros**), park on the right, and look down into the valley for the domed church of Agía Paraskeví, set among the fields beside two cypress trees. This church contains the grave of Yeóryios Khortátzis, a 15th-century local clan leader. A decayed fresco depicts him in armour on horseback taking leave of his wife to fight against the Venetians.

This little church was attached to **Moní Asomáton** monastery, which stands at the crossroads some 3km (2 miles) further down the road. The walled and fortified monastery is now used as an agricultural college, but nobody objects if you go in to the courtyard to look at the 15th-century church whose furnishings are now in the Historical Museum of Crete in Iraklíon (*see p36*).

Turn right in front of the monastery and drive to **Amári**, the modern valley capital. Immediately on entering the village, turn right opposite the police station, following the downhill road to **Agía Anna**. The damaged frescoes in the apse contain an inscription dating them to 1225, making them the oldest firmly dated frescoes on Crete. Emerging from the church there are splendid views across the valley to the mighty Psiloreítis range rising like a cliff. Amári, an unspoilt hilltop village, offers a chance to stop and soak up the rural atmosphere before heading back the way you came to Réthymno, or heading on south, via **Tympáki**, to the cluster of archaeological sites around **Festós** (*see p44 & p90*).

Tour: the Kourtaliotiko Ravine

This short but rewarding drive will take you through a ravine, reminiscent of the famous Samaria Gorge, to Moní Préveli, the monastery overlooking the sea. Take respectable clothes for admission to the monastery but plan to leave them off if you visit the nearby beaches.

Allow at least half a day.

Take the road south out of Réthymno, past the public gardens, signposted to Spíli. After 8km (5 miles), turn right at the signpost to the **Late Minoan**

Cemetery of Arménoi (*open 8am–3pm daily except Mon*). Here are numerous rock-cut tombs dating to the late second millennium BC. The site is covered in orchids and anemones in spring.

Back on the main road continue for 12km (7 miles) and take the right turn, signposted to Plakiás/Préveli Monastery. Soon you will turn a corner to find yourself in the **Kourtaliotiko Ravine**, passing beneath sheer cliffs with the Megapótamos (literally 'Big River') to your left. Part way down the ravine on the left is a layby. If you pull in here you will experience the clattering breeze that gives the ravine its name ('Windy Gorge'), whilst looking up at the cliff faces, pitted with caves and as brown as raw cork bark.

At the southern end of the short ravine, enter Asómatos then turn left for **Moní Préveli** and left again. About 2km (1¼ miles) beyond this last turning you will pass a cooling spot where walkers dip their feet in the Megapótamos near a pretty 19th-century bridge and just before the ruins of the original 16th-century monastery. Its successor, built in the 17th century, lies 4km (2½ miles) further along the narrow winding road, on a clifftop terrace with views to the sea (for the monastery and its museum *see p116*). Driving back to the bridge, a driveable track leads right and along the river to the so-called Palm Beach (*see p117*) but this can be crowded. Other beaches are found by continuing back the way you came and turning left, following signs to **Plakiás**. Beyond Lefkógía, tracks lead left down to a series of pretty coves backed by caves where nobody seems to bother much about wearing any clothes. (Although nudism is prohibited, in remote areas locals may turn a blind eye to it.) Plakiás itself sits in a lovely sheltered bay with sweeping views, and there is a good choice of beachside places to eat and drink.

To return to Réthymno, drive out of Plakiás on the road that brought you in and turn left after 1km (⅔ mile) for **Myrthios**, a pretty village clinging to the mountains overlooking the sea. At the next junction go straight on (not left to Selliá), driving up the steep-sided **Kotsifoú Gorge** (Farángi Kotsifoú). At the next junction go straight on (ignoring the left turn to **Káli Sikía**).

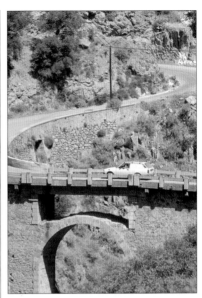

Crossing the ravine

From **Ágios Ioánnis** onwards the road passes through delightful wooded country where cypress trees shade sheep-grazed pastures cut by streams. Just after **Ágios Vasíleios**, turn left to rejoin the main Réthymno road.

Plakiás makes a good spot for lunch

Tour: the Ímvros Gorge

If you are not up to walking the Samaria Gorge there are several possible substitutes, including this lazy way of enjoying the Ímvros Gorge by car.
Allow at least half a day.

Coming from either Chaniá or Réthymno, take the well-signposted turning off the National Highway to **Vrýses** (*see p130*). This attractive town is the meeting point of five roads, and is a popular stopping-off point for hungry travellers. Follow signposts to Chóra Sfakíon through the town and soon you will start to climb towards the Lefká Óri (White Mountains).

After 5km (3 miles) turn left (signposted **Alíkampos**) and, less than 1km (⅖ mile) on, look for a graffiti-covered concrete embankment on a right-turning bend, and turn left down a track to the church of the Panagía. Numerous springs gush out of the hillside and they are channelled into a 16th-century Venetian cistern (restored 1909). A grassy downhill track to the left leads to the church, idyllically set in an orange grove. The frescoes (dated 1315) are some of the best preserved in Crete and depict biblical scenes, from Adam and Eve to the Nativity and Crucifixion (if the church is locked, the friendly priest might be found tending the modern church in Alíkampos, further up the road).

Go back to the main road and turn left, passing through the barren rocky landscape around **Krapis**. Some 5km (3 miles) further on, the scenery changes as you look down to your left, into a neat patchwork of tiny fields with a cone-shaped hill crowned by a circular Turkish fortress. **Ímvros** village marks the beginning of the gorge. From the road you will see little of its stern majesty unless you pull over at one of the numerous viewpoints along the route. The road winds round the top of the cliffs high above the western edge of the gorge. You can, however, descend into the gorge on foot from Ímvros village, following the well-signposted footpath (if you want to walk the whole route, allow 3 hours to reach its southern end (8km/5 miles), and either check the times of return buses before you set out, or arrange for a taxi to collect you).

The road now descends via a series of hairpin bends with far-reaching views to **Chóra Sfakion** (*see p106*), an attractive fishing village where you can enjoy lunch in a taverna set by the side of the crystal-clear sea. The beach here is of shingle – if you fancy a swim, head east on the broad flat coast road to **Fragkokástelo**, where there is a gently shelving child-friendly beach of golden sand and an almost intact 14th-century beachside castle to explore.

For a completely different experience, head west out of Chóra Sfakion on the vertiginous road to **Anópoli**, turning left

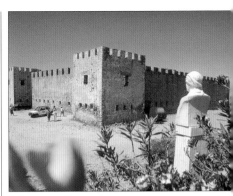

The castle at Fragkokástelo

at the village taverna to follow the new road (not yet shown on all maps) to the village of **Arádiana**. This village, set high above a spectacular ravine, was abandoned some years ago. Left to crumble, the village and surrounding fields give a real sense of Cretan village life as it was before the age of concrete and plastic.

The road follows the cliff tops above the gorge

Getting away from it all

Until the 1970s, Crete had almost no roads, a situation, in Cretan eyes, brought about by their Turkish rulers who deliberately suppressed the island's economy and made no investment in infrastructure. Instead, the island was covered in a network of tracks connecting one village with the next, along which goods were transported by donkey.

Walking is the ideal way to experience the beauty of the Cretan countryside

Supplementing these medieval roads were footpaths, called *kalderími*, paved with the local stone and usually sheltered from the sun by high walls to either side. Where these footpaths survive they nearly always serve to link one church to the next, or a village to its fields, and the walls support a wide variety of plant life.

Walking on Crete

For the tourist, this extensive network provides a great opportunity to explore the island on foot. It is also the best way to admire the rich and varied flora that abounds.

Walking the Kourtaliotiko Ravine: the ruined monastery at Moní Préveli

Walking in Crete is a matter of seeking out the vestiges of this medieval network, though, unfortunately, it is becoming increasingly difficult to do this. The *kalderími* are slowly becoming choked with scrub from lack of use, and tracks are increasingly being concreted over or tarmacked for the benefit of motorists.

Guides and equipment

The presence of tarmac very much depends upon the wealth of the local community: each village pays to have its own roads metalled and, inevitably, it is the poorer inland regions where the tracks survive and where the walking is best. These are also remote regions where help is a long way off if you get into trouble, so basic precautions are essential. Do not set out without telling someone (such as your hotel) where you are going and when you expect to return. Take plenty of water, high-energy food supplies, and protection against the sun, which can be very intense. The best practical guides to exploring Crete on foot are the two pocket books published by Sunflower Books called *Landscapes of Eastern Crete* and *Landscapes of Western Crete* (for maps *see p184*).

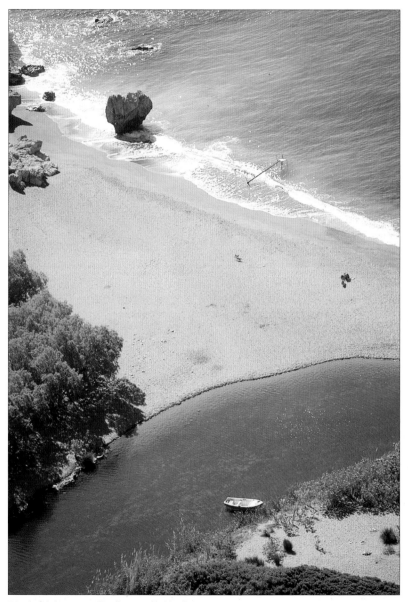

Wonderful views reward walkers on the island

Nature has given Crete colours in abundance – be they those of the delicate orchid. . .

Guided tours

If you want someone else to handle the logistics of getting to and from the start of your walk, consider joining one of the guided tours offered by The Happy Walker, *Odós Tobazi 56, Réthymno (tel: (28310) 52920)*. This organisation offers a different walk each day of around 4 hours' duration, led by a knowledgeable English-speaking guide.

When and where to go

Spring (from April to mid-May) is by far the best time to go walking on Crete because of the sheer wealth of wildflowers and the relatively cool but still pleasant weather.

Autumn (mid-September to October) also brings fine walking weather, but the countryside will be scorched by the summer heat, lacking spring's abundance of colour. The Samaria Gorge is Crete's most famous walk (*see pp126–7*), but as a result of its popularity the path is crowded and noisy: for a quieter and equally magnificent route consider walking the Ímvros Gorge instead (*see p144*).

The south coast offers some excellent walking, using Loutró or Chóra Sfakíon as a base (*see p106*). For more experienced climbers, the Lefká Óri (White Mountains) present a serious challenge. The Kallergi mountain refuge (*tel: (28210) 54560*), open from May to October, is run by the Greek Mountain Club (EOS), and is used by climbers as a base for crossing the range via Páchnes (2,453m/8,048ft), Crete's second-highest peak. Reaching the summit of Crete's highest mountain, Timíos Stavrós (a mere 3m/10ft higher at 2,456m/

8,058ft), is relatively easy for fit and well-equipped climbers by means of a path that leads up from the taverna (closed) to the Ídaean Cave (*see p102*).

THE FLOWERS OF CRETE

Visiting Crete in the summer, it is difficult to imagine just how colourful and rich in wildflowers this stony landscape can be in the spring. Geography and geology combine here to provide a myriad of different ecological niches. The climate varies from the frost-free coastal zone, via the temperate uplands to the alpine slopes of the central mountain ranges. Within these broad divisions, the range of soil types adds to the potential for diversity, and a marked feature of Crete is the local abundance of some plants that are found in one site only, and nowhere else on the island.

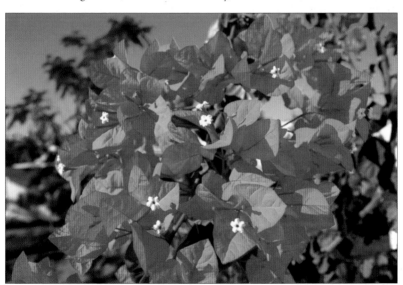

. . . or the vibrant bougainvillaea

When to go

The true wildflower enthusiast will find plants of interest throughout the year. The Cretan spring really begins as far back as October, when heavy rains bring the first crocus and narcissi bursting through the soil, and when the bare earth suddenly turns green almost overnight with new grass and freshly germinated seedlings. For sheer quantity of colour, however, the period from mid-April to mid-May is the main flowering season; this is the time when the slopes of the Lefká Óri range turn from white to red as the snows melt and the scarlet anemones flower.

Where to look

Almost every roadside offers a botanical feast in spring, but for rarer plants – especially orchids and bulbs – you need to head inland from the intensively cultivated coastal plains (where herbicides have, sadly, denuded the fields of their native flora) to the inland and upland regions. Almost any archaeological site will provide rich hunting ground for rare species because (with the exception of Knossós and Festós) these sites are neither ploughed nor sprayed – hence exploring the archaeology of Crete becomes doubly pleasurable because of the wealth of colourful blooms. As an aid to identification, *The Wildflowers of Crete*, an illustrated pocket guide written by George Sfikas, is inexpensive and widely available on the island.

What to look for

Rough uncultivated hillsides abound in various types of spurge, with their vivid

Miniature perfection – the Asiatic buttercup

lime-green flowers, and the thrusting 1-m (3-ft) high spikes of white asphodel. In unsprayed orchards and vineyards, purple oxalis competes with scarlet anemones. Easily mistaken for anemones, but with a lovely powdery sheen and a bell-shaped flower, is the Asiatic buttercup, *Ranunculus asiaticus*, often found on field edges and embankments. *Clematis cirrhosa*, with tiny yellow bellflowers, spotted inside, scrambles all over field walls, as do many pretty bindweeds. The white-flowered Cretan cyclamen blooms in shaded woodland and on damp banks. Among bulbs, irises, crocus, narcissi, lilies and alliums are relatively common, but the little species tulips and the plum-coloured fritillaries are far rarer. Purple- and yellow-flowered orchids are easy to spot in grassland and on uncultivated slopes – though green-, brown- and white-flowered species take some finding amongst the mass of colour.

Wildflower sites

The following sites are especially rich in wildflowers. If you visit them, remember not to disturb the plants in any way, but leave them for future visitors and generations to enjoy.

Eastern Crete

Gortýs (*p48*) is renowned for flowers that seem to grow more luxuriously than elsewhere in this part of the island. Less visited are the flower-covered ruins of the Minoan village of Vasiliki on the western side of the road south from the National Highway to Ierápetra.

Western Crete

Two easily visited sites with abundant wildflowers are the German war cemetery at Máleme (*p110*) and the ancient Minoan cemetery at Arménoi (*p142*). For a longer trip, Polirínia (7km/4½ miles due south of Kastélli) is a marvellous spot for plant hunting. There is an excellent

taverna in the modern village, right next to the beginning of the path that climbs up to the ancient hilltop city, or you can picnic in the ancient olive groves that surround the ruins. Meaning 'rich in lambs', Polirínia was founded in the post-Palatial era (after 1100 BC) and flourished until the Venetian era (13th century), and its substantial remains shelter many kinds of bulbs and orchids.

The Vámos peninsula, especially around Litsárda and Selia, has tiny fields surrounded by drystone walls where rock plants are abundant. The fields, where no longer cultivated, have been colonised by sheets of sky-blue lupins. Anópoli and Arádiana, both accessible by road from Chóra Sfakion (*see p106*), combine an abundance of flowers, growing amongst cherry orchards and olive groves, with extensive coastal views.

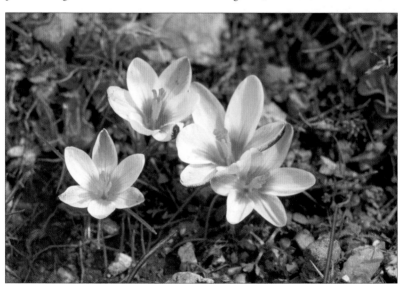

Clusters of crocuses add beauty to the countryside

Shopping

Crete's four provincial capitals offer a huge range of choice, with scores of tiny hole-in-the-wall shops selling handmade leather goods, jewellery, textiles, ceramics and clothing, or village-made organic produce, such as honey, olive oil, dried herbs and nuts. Chaniá and Réthymno are especially pleasant towns in which to shop, because of their characterful traffic-free backstreets and large number of keen young artisans producing imaginative designs.

Sponges are among the bargains to be had in Iraklíon's bustling market

Iraklíon

Head straight for the market in Odós 1866 for the best choice in inexpensive souvenirs. Herbs, leather, Cretan-style leather boots, jewellery, embroidery, dried figs, sponges and loofahs are among the cornucopia of items on offer at good-value prices. If you like Cretan music, look out for the Music Market, on Odós 1821 (the street that runs parallel to the market) or the nearby Record Shop, on the corner of Odós 1821 and Odós 1866, both selling tapes, CDs and videos. Also in Odós 1821 (at No 20) is Nick Papadogiannis, a more upmarket shop dealing in objets d'art – Minoan-style and modern statuary, pottery and jewellery.

Odós Kalokairinou is Iraklíon's principal shopping street – the place to go for clothes and everyday household goods. Odós 25 Augoústou contains a handful of interesting shops amongst the plethora of banks, car hire and travel agents: Eva Grimm (No 6) specialises in old Cretan handicrafts (antique woven cloth and wooden blocks for stamping biscuits, for example); George

Mamouzelos (No 20) has a fascinating collection of sponges, and Minos Cretan Wines (No 12) needs no further explanation.

Fashionable, upmarket clothing stores line the pedestrianised Odós Daidálos, and at the upper end the side streets leading to the Archaeological Museum are dominated by shops selling fine reproductions of Cretan icons and Minoan jewellery and Cycladic sculpture: Galeria Dedalou (Odós Daidálos No 11), Galenté (Odós Sapoutie No 2) and Elene Kastrinoyanni (Platíea Eleftherias No 1) have the widest selections.

Ágios Nikólaos

Cheap souvenir shops dominate this resort, but better quality can be found in the two streets that run uphill from the harbour. Starting with Odós 28 Octóbriou, look for the shop on the right called Marieli which sells tapestries, handmade by the former journalist, Sofia Kana, using only natural dyes, plus modern jewellery, glass and ceramics. At No 14, Byzantio sells handpainted icons that are copied from churches and monasteries. Chez Sonia, at No 20, is another outlet for antique Cretan costumes, and for more unusual contemporary crafts and designs, including tapestries, puppets, ceramics and brasswork. On Odós Roussou Koundoúrou, Marisso (No 21) sells quality jewellery and, next door,

Pegasus sells antique jewellery and modern jewellery incorporating ancient Greek coins. Round the next corner in Odós Sfakionaki, Maria Patsaki has been here for 20 years selling handwoven bedcovers, rugs, carpets, and beautiful fabrics that can be bought by the metre or made up.

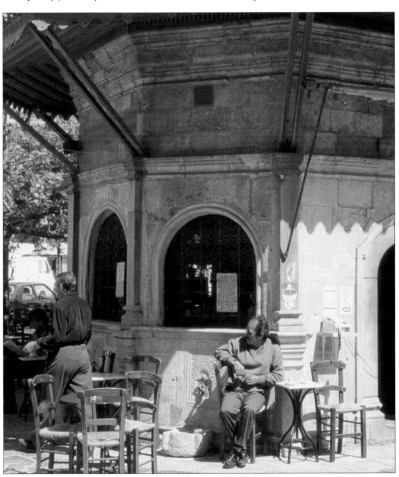

Odós 1866, the market street, leads to this pretty kiosk

Impromptu herb stall: Saturday is often the principal market day

Chaniá

Chaniá market hall makes a good starting point for a shopping expedition, though you may get no further as you linger over stalls laden with cheeses, herbs, honey, fish, fruit, meat and vegetables.

Leather Alley

Even more crowded and tempting is Odós Skridlóf, just down from the market, packed with stalls selling keenly priced leather bags, belts, sandals, wallets and shoes. Dig amongst the stalls and you will find one or two shops that don't sell leather: Tango (No 27) has some unusual jewellery and cast-glass lamps, No 31 sells videos and tapes of Cretan music, and Mares, opposite, sells camping, walking, fishing and snorkelling gear. If you fancy a pair of handmade knee boots, Cretan-shepherd style, look for the boot and shoe shop at No 67, but don't expect these to come cheap – they are made to last a lifetime.

Odós Khalídon

Cheap souvenirs account for most of the shops on this street, but do look out for colourful T-shirts, kaftans and beachwear at Nos 67 and 65. Opposite, Best is a browsing shop, full of colourful jewellery, painted wood toys and boxes, and woven straw hats. In the domed former Turkish bath on the right, you can watch a bronze-caster at work making scales, weights, bells, ornate candlesticks and door knockers. Further down, at No 5, Anatolita sells highly desirable ceramics and jewellery by the French artists, Juliette and Patrick Fabré.

To the fortress

The narrow alleys of the old Venetian quarter leading up to Chaniá's fortress are dotted with shops selling the work of innovative young artists. Just as a sampler, walk up Odós Zambelioú and look for Bizarro, selling wacky waistcoats and blouses, plus exquisite puppets and dolls. Roba Carpets (No 61) sells kilims and carpets made on the loom, and on Odós Angeloú (running left from the entrance to the fortress) don't miss Top Hanao for the best selection of old Cretan rugs and tapestries you are likely to find on the island.

Réthymno

Slightly more expensive and perhaps a touch more upmarket than Chaniá, Réthymno is packed with shopping temptations. Leading up to the castle, Odós Salamínas has attracted young potters, painters and jewellers whose shops line both sides of the street. Below the castle, on Odós Katehaki, Zaharias Theodorakis has his workshop where you can watch him turning onyx by hand to make vases, bowls and lamps. Odós Arambatzoglou is packed with shops such as The Link, for ethnic jewellery, Talisman for hanging lamps, and Dharma for handmade clothes – just right for wearing to the disco. Also here is Olive Tree, selling furniture, jewellery and hair ornaments of olive wood. In Odós Vernadou, which runs parallel, one block south, look for the Old Town Gallery, selling Judith Mooney's atmospheric watercolour paintings of Cretan village life.

Odós Ethníkos Anistáseos is the main shopping street for the townspeople, with a market at its upper end. For something truly local, look for Kogreion (No 41), selling worry beads in every imaginable colour and a ferocious array of knives. No 16 is a Dickensian antique shop where you may pick up an oil lamp amongst the miscellaneous junk. The little lane called Soulion has shops specialising in children's toys in painted wood and handmade dolls in Cretan costume.

Buy direct from the farmer in Ágios Nikólaos

CRETAN CRAFTS

Some Cretan crafts – such as icon
painting and jewellery making – have
been revived in recent times by young,
college-trained Cretans, keen to explore
their ancient Minoan heritage. Their
work is to be found in shops all over
Crete and is remarkably good value,
with jewellery, for example, selling at
prices only a little above the cost of the
raw materials. Other crafts, especially
pottery and weaving, form part of a
living tradition that has never died out,
one that stems back 4,000 years to the
Minoan era.

Shoulder bags, Cretan style

Pottery

Two villages specialise in the
manufacture of pottery using timeless
techniques. The potters of Margarítes,
midway between Iraklíon and Chaniá,
supply many shops in Crete, but you can
buy more cheaply, and watch the pots
being made, by seeking them out at
their source. Vases, and pots intended as
tableware, are glazed a vivid azure blue –
the same blue used for painting the
house exteriors in this unspoiled village.
You can also see a whole range of
humbler stoneware and salt-glazed
vessels – olive jars, bread-kneading
troughs and jugs for olive oil or wine.

Ilias Ceramica, at the entrance to the
town, has the widest selection of pottery
shapes and colours. For giant terracotta
pithoi, just like those found in Minoan
palaces, head on up through the town
and out to the other side to Ceramica
Kallerges (on the right) and Nickos
Kaugalakis (further up on the left).

The other village, Thrapsanó, lies to
the southeast of Iraklíon, near Myrtiá.

Here, the abundant red clay is simply
scooped from the ground, shaped into
giant *pithoi* and fired in wood kilns.
Standing over 1m (3ft) tall, they do not
make ideal souvenirs for carrying home,
but there are lots of smaller pots for sale
in the numerous shops in the village and
lining the Kastélli road.

Weaving

Antique woven cloth and tapestries, if
you can track them down, are richly
coloured from the use of vegetable dyes,
and decorated with simple geometric
designs (good examples are displayed in
the Museum of Cretan Ethnology in
Vóroi – *see p78*). Woven from wool on a
small horizontal loom, textile lengths are
finished by knotting the warp threads
and stitching lengths together to make
bedspreads, knapsacks, saddle cloths
and other items. Many towns in Crete
sell woven bags and wall hangings, but
to see the weavers at work, it is best to
go to Anógia (east of the pottery town
of Margarítes) or to Kritsá, on the hill
to the southwest of Ágios Nikólaos.

The housefronts in both villages are hung from rooftop to pavement level with examples of weaving, and there is more inside. The loom is often situated just inside the front door of the shop, so that the black-clad women weavers can rush out and commandeer any potential customers, sometimes physically pushing and pulling them into the shop while keeping up a stream of sales patter in broken English or German.

Be prepared to be tough-skinned in seeking out precisely what you want and comparing prices before you buy. Do not pay over the odds for mass-produced rugs decorated with motifs from Minoan frescoes, such as leaping dolphins, acrobats and bulls. On the other hand, do not expect genuine handmade textiles to come cheap. If you are easily intimidated by aggressive sales techniques, you may find it more enjoyable to go instead to Top Hanao, the shop in Chaniá that specialises in genuine handwoven rugs and bedspreads.

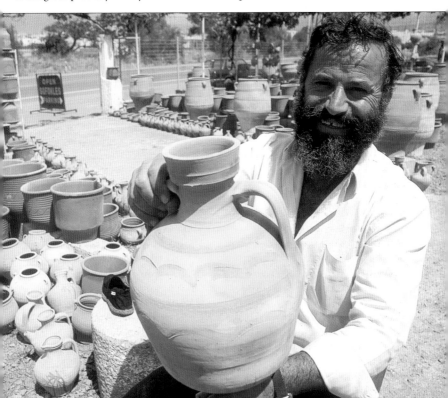

Buy direct from the producers for the best bargains in handmade pottery

Entertainment

Discos are found almost everywhere

Discos abound in Crete's towns and holiday resorts, patronised as much by local youth as by holidaymakers. Other forms of entertainment are far harder to find on Crete, the choice often being limited to drama in the open-air theatres of Réthymno or Iraklíon (incomprehensible if you do not understand Greek), or rather saccharine performances of Cretan music and dance, usually provided as part of a carefully packaged 'Cretan Evening' and heavily promoted by tour agents.

Discos

Cretan discos are pretty relaxed by the standards that prevail in many European cities. Dress codes are unheard of, and there is often only a minimum admission fee – the disco makes its money from the sale of drinks but, this being Crete, the prices are not extortionate by any means. A popular activity is cruising from one disco to the next, looking for the best party atmosphere.

Cretan music

An evening spent listening to authentic Cretan songs, variously jolly and wistful, plaintive and rambunctious, can be a memorable experience (if you drink too much *raki*, as you will surely be encouraged to do, you may also end up with a very memorable headache!). The melody in Cretan music is usually played on the three-stringed lyra, which sounds like a violin, accompanied by the flute, guitar, drum, bagpipes and the lute-like *bouzoúki*. Sometimes the vocalist and lyra throw the tune about,

taking it in turns to weave ever more complex variations, with the other instruments providing a driving rhythm that sounds like an Irish jig gone Arabic. Many tavernas offer live music as a background while you eat, but for a taste of the real thing, head for the Café Crete, also known as the Lyrakia, at Odós Kalergon 22, Chaniá. This very basic hole-in-the-wall café behind the Arsenal is where Chaniá's traditional musicians gather for jam sessions and impromptu dancing. The atmosphere is warm and welcoming, especially on Friday night when hundreds of villagers descend on Chaniá for the next day's big street market.

Dancing

Chaniá is also one of the best places to watch traditional dancing from all over the Greek archipelago. The venue is the Firkás Theatre, the rather grand name given to the inner courtyard of the Old Venetian Fortress at the northwestern tip of the harbour. Performances, lasting two hours, take place on some summer evenings, featuring 32 dances from different parts of Greece, each in appropriate costume. The admission ticket includes free *raki*.

Open-air cinema

Cretans are very fond of the cinema and open-air screenings are commonplace in summer in the outdoor theatres in the fortresses at Chaniá and Réthymno, or in the lee of the city wall below the Archaeological Museum in Iraklíon. Screenings are in the original language, with Greek subtitles. Cretan audiences are very noisy, so you may need to listen hard to hear the dialogue. Look out for fly posters advertising these, and more conventional indoor screenings.

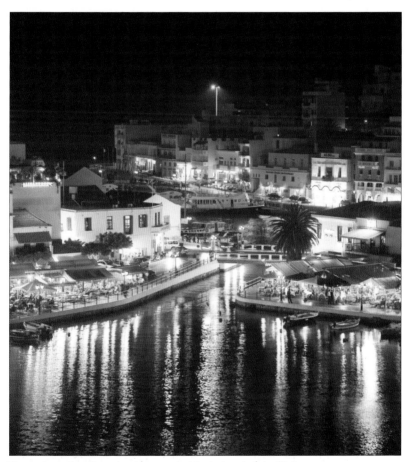

There's plenty of evening entertainment around the harbour in Ágios Nikólaos

C h i l d r e n

Almost nothing on Crete is geared specifically to children's tastes, and yet most children who come to the island on holiday succeed in having a marvellous time. In the process, however, their parents will probably end up being pestered to exhaustion by endless questions provoked by the magical strangeness of everything.

Cafés and tavernas warmly welcome families with children

When visiting Crete with children it is an advantage to choose a resort that has not been swamped by tourism, so that the everyday rhythms and activities of Cretan life can be allowed to take over. Many of the quieter resorts on the south coast – scarcely more than fishing villages – offer safe bathing, traffic-free streets, and the chance to do and see things Cretan. Breakfast on creamy yoghurt flavoured with wildflower honey, shop at the local bakers for fresh bread and syrup-soaked pastries, watch fishermen clean their catch and mend their nets, marvel at the myriad of fish darting among the rock pools by the harbour, and say hello to the laden donkeys as they clip-clop mournfully up the street.

Archaeology and caves

To the horror of purists, most archaeological sites on Crete are unprotected from the erosive effects of visitors' feet and nobody seems to mind that hordes of visitors scramble over 4,000-year-old walls, staircases and courtyards. In fact, short of building a viewing platform above the site, it would be impossible to see the excavated remains without walking all over them.

This presents a great opportunity for children who love exploring ruins and getting lost in the labyrinthine network of streets, corridors and storerooms making up a typical Minoan site. For added gloom, dankness and awesome rock formations, the Díktaean Cave (*see p72*) is a must.

Beaches and watersports

The island offers dozens of sandy beaches and, for older children, a variety of watersports in the main resorts. Undercurrents are quite common and parents should keep a close watch on children swimming in the sea. Care should also be taken to protect children from the sun, particularly between 11am and 3pm when the sun is at its hottest. The island's four waterparks (*see p162*) provide hours of fun for children of all ages.

Boat trips

The seas around Crete are normally as calm as a pond (though they get rough as autumn sets in, from mid-October, and can continue choppy well into April). Well worth considering are the boat excursions from Ágios Nikólaos or Eloúnta out to Spinalónga Island (*see p76*), or the south-coast ferry service linking Palaióchora, Soúgia, Agía Rouméli, Loutró and Chorá Sfakion. For something less adventurous, but equally rewarding, go to Georgioúpoli (*see p130*) and hire a pedal boat for exploring the Almirós River, with its terrapins, crabs and rich bird life.

Food

Cretans love young children and there is no better way of ensuring indulgent service in tavernas than turning up with yours in tow. They are quite likely to be whisked off to the kitchens and introduced to all the members of the taverna owner's extended family. Despite the language barrier, you may find that your children have become firm friends with those of the taverna owner before too much time passes, guaranteeing that you and they are treated like old friends. Few tavernas serve special children's dishes but most menus feature pizza, pasta, omelettes, chicken and chips.

Though few areas cater specifically to children, Crete is packed with magical adventures

Sport and leisure

In the heat of a Cretan summer, few visitors to the island come with the objective of working out and limbering up. Crete caters more for the beach-loving sybarite than the fitness freak. However, organised sports are becoming available and many new pursuits, including golf, are planned to encourage tourists to come to Crete in winter.

Sun and sand: but be careful not to overdo it

Waterparks

There are now four waterparks to choose from, all offering a range of waterslides and other aquatic activities. Chersonísou, east of Iraklíon, has two: Star Beach Waterpark (*tel: (28970)* *24472*) on Beach Road, with numerous sports facilities (waterskiing, windsurfing, parasailing and scuba diving among them) as well as rides, and Aqua Splash (*tel: (28970) 24950*), located just to the north of Chersonísou

Organised fun and excitement for those who prefer it

on the Kastélli road. Midway between
Iraklíon and Chersonísou at Anópoli,
Water City (*tel: (2810) 781316*) has 23
water slides. The latest waterpark is
Limnou Polis (*tel: (28210) 33202*) at
Vathýpetro, 8km (5 miles) southwest
of Choriá.

Diving
The seas surrounding Crete are still
relatively clean and teeming with fish, as
anyone can tell just by looking into rock
pools. Added to this, the sea floor is
covered in antiquities, and because of
this, diving is very strictly controlled.
Among the organisations licensed to
train divers and take them on
recreational trips to the seabed are
Atlantis Diving Centre based at the
*Grecotel, Adeloanos Kampos, Réthymno
(tel: (28310) 78002)*, and the Scuba
Kreta Diving Club at *Nana Beach Hotel,
Chersonísou (tel: (28970) 24076)*. Both
provide English-speaking trainers and
guides and offer introductory dives
of half a day or a day's duration or four-
day courses leading to the
internationally recognised PADI
diving diploma.

Beaches and watersports
Calm waters and lack of wind do not
make the ideal conditions for
windsurfing, but equipment can be
hired from local shops or from
beachside huts in Almrída (*see
pp130–31*) and Chersonísou (near
Mália). In Palaióchora, the English-
run Westwind Windsurfing School
(located in a group of huts on the
north end of the western beach) will
supply boards, tuition and wetsuits,

Natural pleasures abound in Crete

and they run their own rescue boat
service.

Beach and watersport activities on
Crete, in general, depend upon
entrepreneurial young Cretans
(sometimes Germans or English)
setting up a makeshift stall on the beach
for the season. The situation differs
from year to year, but you are almost
certain to find somebody offering the
questionable pleasures of 'banana' rides,
waterskiing and paragliding if you
head for the major resort beaches of
Mália, Ágios Nikólaos or the resort
strip west of Chaniá.

Beach etiquette
Topless bathing is widespread on Cretan
beaches, and nude bathing, although
officially illegal, is commonplace in the
less accessible coves and beaches of the
south coast. If in doubt, take your cue
from the behaviour of others on the
beach. Once off the beach, however, you
are expected to dress with decorum, and
not upset local sensibilities by walking
around in revealing beachwear.

The Cretan diet is the healthiest in the Western world – and that's official. Medical studies into the Mediterranean diet were actually conducted on Crete, where it was found that people lived longer, were healthier in old age, and suffered from less heart disease and cancer than in other parts of Europe and the Americas. The principal components of this diet, until quite recently, were bread in very large quantities, accompanied by olives, lots of fresh fruit and raw vegetables, olive oil, red wine, and protein in small quantities, principally in the form of goat's milk, cheese, walnuts or fish.

Tavernas

The legacy of this peasant diet can still be found on the menu of a typical Cretan taverna where you can eat heartily, and cheaply, on Greek salad (tomatoes, onions, cucumber, olives and feta – sheep's milk cheese), followed by fresh fish, or any number of healthily lean high-fibre dishes, such as stuffed vine leaves (*dolmadákia*), bean soup (*soupa fassólia*) or so-called field vegetables (*agria hórta*), a salad made of wild leaves, most of them related to the dandelion.

'Comfort food'

Fortunately Cretan tavernas also offer a lot of comforting food as well: spinach and cheese pies (*spanakopopita/tiropitakia*) wrapped in filo pastry and oozing with flavour (and fat), for example, or macaroni and minced beef (*pastítsio*) baked with a rich cheese sauce, or aubergine and minced lamb *moussaka*.

Grilled foods

Charcoal-grilled lamb, chicken, pork chops and steak are commonplace, but *souvláki* remains the all-time favourite taverna dish, usually consisting of a barbecued pork kebab, though these days you will also find beef, lamb, mixed meats and fish *souvláki* on most menus. Country tavernas may offer rustic dishes, such as casserole of rabbit (*kounéli*), pigeon (*pitsounia*) or wild boar (*agrióhiros*), whilst every beachside restaurant worthy of its name will offer a tempting choice of grilled fresh fish, such as bream, bass, mullet, snapper, swordfish and (usually imported) lobster.

Sticky desserts

Tavernas do not, as a rule, serve desserts, though most will provide a bowl of delicious yoghurt with honey if asked, or a selection of fruit. For *baklavás* (filo pastry stuffed with honey and nuts) or *kadaifi* (shredded pastry filled with walnuts and syrup) it is traditional to move on to a specialist pastry shop cum café, known as a *zakaroplasteíon*. Here the cloying sweetness of the sticky pastries can be tempered by a strong Greek coffee (*métrio*, for medium sweet, *varí glikó* for sweet, *skéto* for without sugar), or a 'Nescafé' (the all-purpose term for all brands of instant coffee) served cold with a head of whipped milk, or hot with boiled milk.

Alcohol

Retsina – white wine flavoured with pine resin – is an excellent accompaniment to Cretan food, but it is not a traditional Cretan wine. Some rural restaurants serve their own delicious home-made wine, drawing it directly from huge wooden barrels. Bottled local wines include Cava d'Or, Olympias, Gorthys, Tsantalia and Calliga, all of which are available in red, white or rosé versions. Cretan wine makers distil delicious *raki*, a clear brandy-like spirit, from the grape pips and skins left over from the wine-making process. An *ouzeri*, similar to a traditional café (*kafeníon*), serves the aniseed-flavoured aperitif known as *oúzo*, usually with little dishes of olives, cucumber and tomatoes, or beans as an accompaniment.

Left: a typical Cretan dish
Below: your choice of oúzo

F o o d   a n d   d r i n k

Everywhere you go in Crete, even in the remotest villages, you are sure to find a simple taverna serving inexpensive home-cooked food, open from breakfast time to late at night. Tavernas are ubiquitous, but do not expect any great variety amongst the dishes on offer: menus are virtually identical, from one end of the island to the other.

Fish, part of the national staple diet

How, then, do you select a taverna, especially when faced with the plethora of choice that exists in the popular resorts and in the harbour areas of Chaniá and Réthymno? Start by ignoring any restaurant that employs touts to attract custom, and treat with suspicion any that display glossy pictures illustrating the dishes on offer. These tourist tavernas are, on the whole, more expensive and worse value than the simple unpretentious tavernas used by local people. If you want a hearty Greek salad that clearly hasn't been portion-controlled, or a generous-sized swordfish steak, instead of a piece the size of a postage stamp, avoid the tourist areas. Be prepared to sacrifice the harbour views in favour of better value and better cooking in the backstreets and side alleys.

Menus

Restaurants in big towns will usually present a multilingual menu, but in village tavernas you may simply be taken to the kitchen and shown what is available. Menus will usually indicate whether fish is fresh or frozen. Most fresh fish is priced by the kilo and can be very expensive if you choose exotic varieties, such as lobster, but very good value if

you stick to local fish. A red mullet or red snapper, for example, typically weighing 0.75kg (1½lb), makes a substantial and inexpensive meal for two.

Booking

Nobody bothers to book tables in Crete and space will always be found for newcomers, even if it means bringing extra tables and chairs out. In any event, there is always another almost identical taverna next door.

Prices

Just as menus vary little, so prices are consistent across the island. The price of the meat will vary according to what you eat rather than where, with fresh fish being more expensive than meat, and baked or stuffed dishes being cheapest of all.

Some restaurants, especially those located in the provincial capitals, are trying to move upmarket, offering a more formal ambience than the traditional taverna. These are slightly more expensive and are indicated in the text by a ★★ symbol (three-course meal for two with local wine costing up to €26) as opposed to the ★ symbol (the same for up to €17).

Vegetarian food

Although Cretan food is dominated by fish and meat dishes, there are usually vegetarian options on most menus. Dishes like *briam* (a kind of ratatouille) and stuffed tomatoes, stuffed peppers and aubergines are all very tasty. Be sure to check they don't have meat in them, though, as they can be cooked both ways. No Cretan menu is complete without a long list of salads, either.

IRAKLÍON

For all its size, Iraklíon does not have a huge choice of restaurants. For best value, head for Fotíou Theodosáki, the alley linking Odós 1866 and Odós Evans. The numerous and nameless tavernas here are busy with market customers and traders during the day and serve authentic Cretan baked dishes and roast meats.

Giovanni ★★

Typically Cretan, set in a quiet back lane dripping with bougainvillaea, just off Odós Daidálou. Candlelit interior or tables in the street. *Odós Koraí 12.*

Ionia ★★

Popular with archaeologists since it was founded in 1923, the Ionia serves traditional Greek fare. The menu is based on what is fresh in the nearby market. *Odós Evans 3.*

Ippokambos ★

Popular taverna near the harbour with excellent-value fish dishes and a large choice of *mezédes* (snacks with drinks). *Sófokli Venizélou.*

Loukoulos ★★

Serves a good range of authentic pizzas, cooked in a wood-fired brick oven, plus fish and vegetarian dishes. *Odós Koraí 5.*

O Kyriakos ★★

Smart and formal place, popular for special occasions. The *meze* spread is highly recommended. *Odós Leofóros Dimokratías 53.*

Pagopoleion ★★

International menu with casseroles, steaks and burgers. Pretty

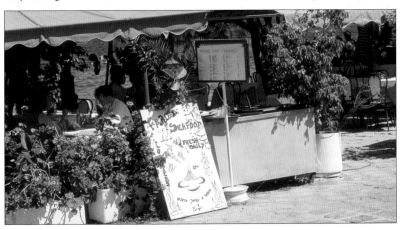

Seafood right by the sea, a Cretan treat

setting on Ágios Títos square. Music in the evenings.
Plateía Ágios Títos.

Psaria ★★
Situated at the harbour end of this busy street, some tables enjoy good views down over the fortress, but there is a lot of traffic noise. The salads and seafood can be excellent, but popularity has led to offhand service.
Odós 25 Augoústou.

Tartuffo ★/★★
The wood-oven pizzas are worth the ten-minute walk from the centre of town.
Leofóros Dimokratías 83.

Taverna Paralia ★
Right by the water with views of the Venetian fortress, one of the best places to try fresh fish (and not too expensively). *Odós Venizélou 5.*

Terzakis ★
The kind of backstreet basic *ouzerie* that is so popular these days, and that casual visitors seldom find. Check off what you want from the list of *meze* the waiter brings round. *Odós Marineli 17.*

Vizandio ★
The pavement tables sheltered by (plastic) vines and (real) bougainvillaea spill round into pedestrianised Odós Daidálou. Serves everything from inexpensive pasta and pizza to veal dishes and grilled meats.
Odós Byzántiou.

EASTERN CRETE
Agía Galíni
The little resort of Agía Galíni, about halfway along the south coast, has lots of good eating places. Below are just two of the best.

Charlie's Place ★
Fun place with bags of character, which doesn't even have a phone. Small menu but creative Cretan dishes.

Madame Hortense ★★
Some of the best food in town (try their chicken with peas and olives), and tables overlooking the harbour are in great demand so get there early.

Ágios Giórgios
Dias ★ and Rea ★
Situated on the main street, these two restaurants serve local dishes (rabbit in season) and village wine, and make a good alternative to the more crowded restaurants of nearby Psychró.

Ágios Nikólaos
Tourist-trap restaurants line the harbour and the south side of Lake Voulisméni. As always, the more interesting restaurants are located a block or so back from the seafront.

La Casa ★
Seating by the lake and a menu ranging from simple snacks to full meals make this a very popular spot. *28 Oktovriou 31.*

Meltemi ★★
Classy dining in the award-winning restaurant at the Istron Bay Hotel – worth the short drive out of town south along the coast to sample the imaginative cooking.
Istron Bay Hotel.

Pelagos ★★
Excellent fish tavern set in a neoclassical mansion, with a fishing boat in the front garden. Dine in the attractive rear garden. Good-value *fruits de mers* (seafood salad). *Odós Koráka 9.*

Zefiros ★★
Lively spot serving all the typical Cretan dishes.
At the start of Aktí Koundoúrou (the seafood promenade).

Eloúnta

Eloúnta's seafront is lined with restaurants all serving the same fish menus. The prices here, reflecting the cost of fresh seafood, tend to be higher than in many parts of Crete, but you can stick to pasta or omelette for a budget meal, or go to the big and boisterous **Ferryman ★**
At the southern end of the waterfront, the Ferryman's menu is more imaginative than most in this resort. Try the Cretan lamb in red wine. *Waterfront.*

Poulis ★★
A typical Eloúnta restaurant offering mixed fish platter (lobster, red mullet, squid, octopus, swordfish and sole).

Vritomartes ★★
Built on an artificial island in the harbour, less pricey than some, and selling more unusual types of fish caught by the restaurant's own boat.

Ierápetra

Just up from the Venetian fortress, on Odós Samóyha, is **Phesteria ★** tavern, which prides itself on fresh fish grilled over charcoal. Further up the same street, all with beachside tables, are the **Ouseri Manos**, **Kyknos**, **Konaki**, **Napoleon** and **Sea Horse** (all ★), serving standard taverna fare at reasonable prices.

Káto Zákros

Káto Zákros Bay Restaurant ★
Family taverna right by the sea in this idyllic little spot, using ingredients from their own farm.

Mália

Huge numbers of tavernas line the main street of this popular resort, most offering Cretan food tailored to British tastes. For something more authentic, head for nearby **Mílatos**, which has several very simple but good, reasonably priced restaurants serving fresh fish.

Mátala

The lovely beachfront is lined with west-facing tavernas, all with terraces designed to make the most of the views and the soothing sound of the breaking waves. All the tavernas specialise in fresh fish and there is little to choose between them. **Sirlaki ★**, situated on the beach, has a huge menu of pizzas, pasta, Greek dishes, grilled meat or fish and offers wine from the barrel. The less-accessible **Skala ★** fish taverna, situated just across the cliffs, is smaller and cheaper.

An innovative sign to catch your attention

TAVERNA "VRITOMARTES"
φρεσκα ψαρια
απο τα ψαροκαϊκα μας

Myrtos

Taverna Akti ★

Fresh fish brought to your table, or slightly unusual dishes like octopus *stifadi*, set this taverna apart. It's at the far eastern end of the string of waterfront tavernas.

Sitía

Creta House ★

Real Cretan cooking, aimed at locals all year round and not just summer tourists. *Odós Karamánli.*

Mixos ★

Much liked by locals, with imperious and unsmiling waiters (all part of the act) serving excellent mixed grilled fish and chicken, spit-roasted over a glowing charcoal fire. Tables spill out onto the street in summer.
Odós Kornarou 112.

Zorbas ★

This huge taverna, with tables on the harbour and round two other sides of the block, nevertheless offers snappy service. Visitors come to enjoy huge plates of mixed *souvláki* or mixed grilled fish and to enjoy the bustling atmosphere.
Odós Venizélou 64.

Tzermiádo

Kri-Kri ★

Distinguishes itself from the other tavernas in town by serving freshly cooked food (not cooked earlier and warmed up) along with home-made wine served from the barrel.
On the main street.

Kronio ★

Authentic Greek fare including *stifado* (meat stew), lamb with arti-chokes, *dolmades* (stuffed vine leaves), and cuttle fish with spices.
In the centre of the village.

WESTERN CRETE
Chaniá

Chaniá is the gourmet capital of Crete, with scores of good tavernas lining the long harbour front, and as many more in the characterful alleys of the old city beneath the fortress. The waterfront restaurants divide roughly into three sections. Nearest the fortress (on Aktí Kountourioti) are the young, noisy, popular and reasonably cheap tavernas. Beyond the Mosque of the Janissaries (on Aktí Tombázi) are the quieter, more sophisticated (and expensive) places.

Around and beyond the Arsenal buildings (on Aktí Enoseos) come the tavernas most favoured by local people – more typically Cretan in the informal and friendly management style (and occasionally offering dishes you will not find elsewhere, such as salads made of wild leaves).

Amphora ★

One of the best on the harbour, with an excellent spread of *meze* and good fresh fish. *Aktí Kountourioti 49.*

Aposteles ★

Locally favoured taverna serving unusually generous fish portions.
Junction of Aktí Enoseos and Odós Sarpidóna.

Arti ★★

Elegant, candlelit bistro with international menu. Swiss and German run.
Skoufon 15.

Dinos ★★

Justifiably popular seafood taverna. Fine views of the harbour.
At the far eastern end of the Venetian harbour, on the corner with Odós Sarpidóna.

Kariatis ★

Good-value pizzeria and spaghetteria favoured by students at the local Technical University.
Behind the Customs House in Plateía Katehaki.

Karnáyo ★

Very popular with locals, with an extensive menu that includes such exotica as snails and sea urchins (or, as the menu graphically calls them, 'sea hedgehogs').
Plateía Katehaki (the square beside the Arsenal building and Customs House).

Mikalis ★★

Classy Cretan cuisine on a terrace overlooking the outer harbour, with country dishes like snails and Cretan sausages. *Aktí Tombázi.*

Niktenda ★★

Well worth the taxi ride from Chaniá, both for the food and garden setting. Occasional local music and dancing.
Korákies (a village 5km/3 miles east of Chaniá).

Semiramis ★

Atmospheric place with a big garden for eating out of doors and live Cretan music 6.30–10.30pm nightly.
Odós Skoufon.

Suki Yaki ★★

Despite a Japanese-sounding name, Suki Yaki is an upmarket Chinese restaurant (also serving Thai dishes to add to the ethnic confusion).
Odós Hálidan (next to the Archaeology Museum). Dinner only.

Sultanas ★

This colourful restaurant, hung with tapestries and carpets, occupies the former harem of a Turkish official and prides itself on home-style cooking.
Odós Moskon (next to the Ranieri Gate).

Tamam ★★

Popular taverna converted from the old Turkish baths. Basement interior is simple but atmospheric. Tables spill on to the pavement in summer. Cheap house wine straight from the barrel.
Odós Zambelioú. Dinner only.

To Hani Garden Restaurant ★

Specialises in more unusual Cretan dishes, such as *tsigariasto* (a Sfakiot goat-meat dish), *tourla* (lamb and cheese pie) and *dakos* (a salad of cheese, tomatoes and rusk). For parties of 12 who order 24 hours in advance, they will serve a Cretan Pilaf, a magnificent feast of rice and herb-stuffed mountain lamb. Live music nightly, 6pm to midnight.
Odós Kondiláki 26.

Several restaurants in Chaniá have attractive patios or courtyard gardens

Well of the Turk ★★
Cellar taverna with spicy food and Arabic music.
Kalinikou Zarpáki 1 (just north of the market).

Georgioúpoli
Almiros ★
The town's best restaurant, with an extensive range of good-value dishes.
On the south side of the main square.
Captain ★
Charcoal-grilled dishes and *giros* (doner kebabs).
On the north side of the main square.
Poseidon ★
Rough and ready taverna, reached down a 100-m (330-ft) long path, serving absolutely fresh fish caught by local fishermen.
On the right-hand side of the road leading out to the National Highway.

Kolymvári
Locals come to Kolymvári from all over Crete for seafood dishes. Try the **Spatha** ★★ taverna (on the eastern side of the main square), with its garden terrace and sea views, or the **Diktina** ★ and **Argedina** ★ tavernas, facing each other further

north on the Moní Gonías road, beyond the post office.

Palaióchora
Many of Palaióchora's restaurants are grouped round the central crossroad and the tables spill over the narrow pavements onto the road, causing havoc if any vehicle tries to get through.
Akropolis Ouzeri ★
A thoroughly Cretan establishment, very plain and functional, serving local sausages and rabbit.
On the crossroad in the centre of the town.
Caravella ★
Specialises in freshly caught fish with tables right on the foreshore.
By the ferry harbour.
Christos ★
Fresh fish or roast lamb.
Odós Venizélou, just before the tourist information centre.
Elite ★
Worth seeking out on Saturday nights for its Cretan music and dancing.
At the far end of the western beach road, beyond the Hotel Elma.
Galaxy Fish Restaurant ★★
In a place like this all you need to see on the menu

is 'fresh fish from Palaióchora' to know it should be good, and it is. Ask to see the day's catch and they'll bring it to the table for you. It's opposite the pebble beach at the eastern end of town.
The Third Eye ★
Imaginative vegetarian dishes.
Close to the westernmost of the two beaches.

Réthymno
Avoid the multitude of overpriced restaurants lining the Aktí Venizélou beach road, and head for the Venetian Harbour, where there is a good choice of seafood restaurants, or the alleys leading off Odós Arambatzoglou, where the pavement tables turn the whole area into one big outdoor party at night.
Avli ★★
Very elegant restaurant within an old Venetian manor house. Try baby lobster in shrimp sauce, baked lamb in egg lemon sauce and casseroled goat. Delightful courtyard meals alfresco.
Odós Xanthoudídou 22.
Cava d'Oro ★
Perhaps the best of a run of seafood restaurants on

the Venetian Harbour. Standard fare here is 'Fisherman's Platter' – mixed grilled fish with mussels, shrimps and squid.

At the Customs House end of the Venetian Harbour.

Famagusta ★

Try this Cypriot-owned restaurant if you are fed up with the usual Cretan dishes. As well as Cypriot dishes (such as *sheftalia* – meat balls served with yoghurt), curries, stir-fried dishes and Japanese *teriyaki* are on the menu, and the special list of children's dishes features home-made fish fingers. *Plateía Plastera 6 (west of the Venetian Harbour).*

Fanari ★

Slightly away from the hectic inner harbour and more relaxing, the Fanari does first-class grilled meat and the house wine is very tasty. *Kefalogiáni 16.*

Kyria Maria ★

Real home-cooking from the Maria in the name – don't miss her lamb *kleftiko* if it's on the menu. *Moshovítou 20.*

O Gounas ★

Plain and hearty Greek fare, but the big attraction is the Cretan music, into the small hours every night. *Koroneou 6.*

Ziller's ★★

Specialises in fillet steak in a number of different guises, but also does excellent grilled octopus and seafood dishes. *Plateía Plastera 8.*

Vámos Peninsula

Demetros ★

Fresh fish served on a terrace literally feet away from the sea, a romantic (and peaceful) spot at night.

Almyrída, north of Kalíves.

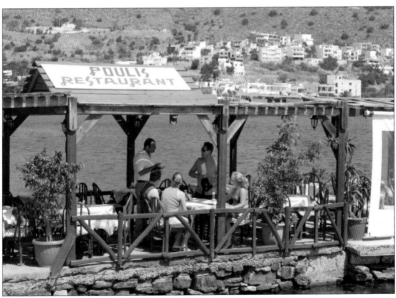

A waterside restaurant in Eloúnta

Hotels and accommodation

Crete offers a huge range of accommodation, from simple 'rent rooms' in someone's home to luxurious self-contained resorts with private beaches, shops, restaurants, and sports facilities. Most middle-range accommodation is located in small hotel or villa complexes where you can expect a simply furnished room with en-suite shower and toilet, a balcony for enjoying the sun, and sometimes a small kitchen for preparing light meals.

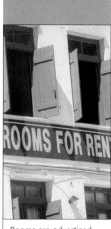

Rooms are advertised with eye-catching signs

Hotels

Greek hotels are classified into six categories (luxury, A, B, C, D and E) according to the standard of facilities and services on offer. Unless you want to live in the lap of luxury, A and B class hotels are adequate and comfortable. Room prices are fixed according to the hotel's classification, but hoteliers will often (quite legitimately) get round this by charging for a whole range of extras, especially during the high season. You may find, for example, that the hotel charges you extra if you only stay one night; it can also insist on charging you for breakfast, or even for half board (breakfast and either lunch or dinner) even if you do not want to eat in the hotel. The lower-category hotels do not usually have restaurants and so cannot do this. Some will levy a charge for supplying a television in your room or present you with a bill for electricity consumed by central heating or air-conditioning systems, so make sure you know what the likely cost is to be in advance.

Villas and self-catering

Many package-tour companies offer accommodation in villa complexes rather than hotels, and these are not subject to the same degree of government control, so you cannot always be sure of the facilities on offer. A key point to check before you book is the availability of heating and air conditioning. Many villas have no heating, and this can result in a miserable holiday spent searching for warmth if, as can happen in April and October, cold wet weather sets in. Conversely, you may be glad of something more than an open window for keeping cool during the intense heat of a Cretan summer.

Rent Rooms

Private accommodation, known universally on Crete as 'Rent Rooms', can be had in every tiny village. Traditionally, the family rented out spare rooms in their homes, but today's rent rooms are more likely to be in purpose-built blocks, equipped with kitchens and showers. Prices vary greatly, so you should shop around. It is accepted that you will want to see your room before agreeing to take it, and bargaining over the price is normal practice during the less busy seasons. Best discounts are given to people who intend to stay three days or more, and some owners may not be willing to rent rooms for a stay of only one night.

Go as you please
Most visitors to Crete base themselves in one place for a week or more, and travellers touring the island, staying at a different place each day, are still something of an oddity. Touring during the high season (July, August and early September) is made more difficult by the fact that most accommodation is pre-booked by tour operators. Touring in the spring and autumn is perfectly feasible, however, and you can sometimes secure big discounts on room rates from hoteliers keen for your custom.

Camping
There are about 20 official campsites on Crete (see *http://interhike.com* for details), and the standard is generally good. Legally you must use an official campsite, but in practice many visitors camp rough, near beaches and so on. It is not usually a problem, provided you are discreet, but there are occasional clampdowns and you must move on to an official campsite if instructed by the police.

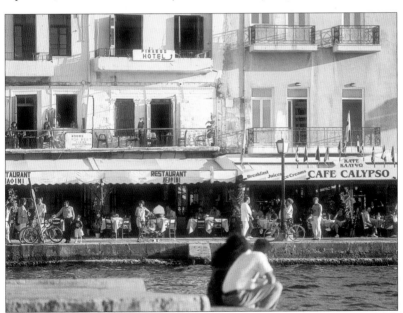

The cheapest hotel may be above a busy restaurant: backstreets could be quieter

On business

Despite the warmth and genuine friendliness of Cretan hospitality, Crete remains a closed society, almost impossible for non-Cretans to penetrate when it comes to business. Almost invariably, those foreigners who have succeeded in establishing businesses in Crete have done so by marrying a Cretan and 'going native'.

Banks will help you through the maze

Crete has only very recently emerged from the pre-industrial age, and though flashy types in BMWs are common enough in the provincial capitals, rural Crete still has a peasant economy, based on self-sufficiency and barter, rather than monetary exchange.

Tourist-fuelled growth
All this is changing because of tourism, which has brought rich, free-spending visitors to the island in ever-increasing numbers since the 1970s.

Tourism is overtaking agriculture as the main source of income for the islanders; and in the island's plan for year-round tourism the number of annual visitors is on the rise.

The chief beneficiaries of tourism have been the owners of property or land in the coastal regions, which attract the maximum number of holiday-makers, and where the landscape has been transformed by hotel building.

Being self-sufficient in many important resources, including building materials, Crete has rapidly developed its tourist infrastructure without building up huge trade deficits – in fact, it imports very little (except for fuel, vehicles and industrial metals).

Agriculture
Crete has a healthy export trade, exploiting its abundant sunshine and fertile soils to grow citrus fruits, bananas, peppers, tomatoes, aubergines and cucumbers, gaining a premium price for these products in winter, when out-of-season salad crops are scarce.

Environmental issues
The income from intensive horticulture is slowly bringing benefits to the once-isolated southern coast of Crete, though not without controversy.

As visitors to the major archaeological sites at Festós and Gortýs will discover, vast areas of the southern coastal plain are disappearing beneath a sea of plastic, as more and more farmers build polythene greenhouses to protect and warm their crops. Worse still, from an environmental point of view, unscrupulous landowners have deliberately set off major forest fires on the south of the island.

Towards integration
In theory, Crete should become increasingly more open to foreign investment and overseas business involvement, now that, as part of

Greece, it is a member of the European Union. Overseas banks have in fact started to open branches in Iraklíon, the capital, in anticipation of this, and anyone planning to do business in Crete would do well to contact these banks for assistance.

Greece as a whole is currently promoting itself as a conference venue, upgrading facilities and infrastructure.

Hotels provide the main bulk of conference venues and this is particularly true of Crete. One of the most desirable and best equipped on the island is the Capsis Beach Resort Hotel, 25km (16 miles) west of Iraklíon (*tel: (2810) 811112; fax: (2810) 811076*). For detailed information on all conference venues on the island, contact your Greek National Tourist Office (*see p188*).

The pace of life and business in Crete can be slow

Practical guide

Arriving
By air
Scores of tour operators sell package tours to Crete and this is by far the cheapest way of getting to the island. Flight-only deals on charter flights are also available. Scheduled flights into Crete are expensive and involve a change of plane and terminal at Athens' airport. Because the island is so well served by package operators, budget airlines don't fly there. Check *www.flythomascook.com* for flights to Iraklíon. Alternatively, consider arriving in Crete the traditional way – by ferry from Piréas (the port of Athens).

Visas
US, Commonwealth and European Union nationals can stay in Crete for up to three months without a visa. Officially, to stay longer, you should apply to the tourist police for a visa, providing evidence that you can support yourself. Few people bother, since the checks on leaving Crete are minimal – even if you are fined for overstaying, the amount of money involved is negligible.

Airport facilities
The main point of entry is the airport at Iraklíon, 5km (3 miles) east of the city centre. Rebuilt in 1995, this is a modern, relatively efficient airport with the usual facilities.

A few tour operators also use the small, recently upgraded airport near Chaniá. This is useful if you are staying in the west of the island. The airport at Sitía, in the east, is slowly being expanded.

Onward travel
Tour operators meet their customers at the airport and arrange onward travel by coach or taxi. If you are on your own, you can also take a taxi – the fares from the airport to the main destinations around the island are fixed, but it is wise to double-check and agree the fare in advance to avoid arguments at the other end. From Iraklíon airport buses leave every few minutes for the city centre; from Chaniá airport buses meet incoming flights, but many people take taxis.

By sea
Separate ferries ply daily across the Sea of Crete between the ports of Piréas and Iraklíon, Chaniá and Réthymno. Minoan high-speed ferries now take only six hours to Piréas and, if you are touring Greece, this is a remarkably cheap way to bring your car across. Travel agents in any Greek city will handle bookings – be sure to get the direct sailings, rather than those that stop at various islands, unless you want to double the journey time.

The Thomas Cook publication *Greek Island Hopping* has details of ferry times and can be purchased from *www.thomascookpublishing.com*, Thomas Cook branches in the UK or by telephoning *00 44 1733 416477*.

Camping
Crete has some 20 or so official camping sites, graded A (luxury) to C (basic), and a complete list can be obtained from tourist offices in Crete. You need not limit yourself to these, however, because

although camping in the wild is against the law in Greece, plenty of enterprising farmers and landowners have put up 'Camping' signs on their land (especially on the roads leading to the popular beaches). In return for a small fee they will supply water and use of a kitchen, toilet and shower.

Children
Children are universally adored in Crete and taking yours on holiday will guarantee that you make lots of friends. On the other hand, Cretan children are treated as mini-adults, expected to eat the same food, and stay up as late as grown-ups. Children's menus in tavernas are not common, but there is usually something they will readily eat (*see also p160*).

Climate
The peak tourist season, from June to September, is very hot and dry, and the sun is intense. Cretans stay indoors for the hottest part of the day and cover up when they go out, to prevent sunburn. Spring (April and May) is delightful, with flower-filled meadows and warm, but not searing, sunshine.

Autumn begins in October and is marked by occasional downpours that can last a day or an hour, interspersed by days of brilliant blue skies and sunshine. Visiting Crete at this time of year can be a gamble because of the rain, but the island is becoming more popular as a winter-holiday destination, where it is possible to ski in the mountains during the day and eat outdoors by the coast in the evening – in winter the temperature by the sea rarely drops below 8°C (46°F) and is often considerably warmer.

Conversion tables
See p181.
Clothes and shoe sizes in Crete generally follow the standard sizes used in the rest of Europe.

Crime
Blissfully, Crete is relatively crime-free, and the only antisocial behaviour you are likely to encounter is from other visitors. Even here, the lager louts stick to their own haunts, and if you avoid late-night bars you are not likely to be troubled by their hooligan behaviour.

Despite the lack of crime, you should not be complacent – look after your valuables and do not leave them where a thief might be tempted; you can always use the hotel lockers.

IRAKLÍON

October–January

May–August

Weather Conversion Chart
25.4mm = 1 inch
°F = 1.8 x °C + 32

Customs

There are no customs restrictions on the import and export of duty-paid purchases between Crete and other parts of the European Union. Be sure to check the customs regulations for your own part of the world before travelling. Some countries, including the USA, have far stricter limits on what may be imported from Crete.

Cycling

Crete is becoming increasingly popular among the mountain-bike fraternity, with plenty of testing dirt roads, as well as rock-paved tracks to explore. Mountain bikes can be hired in all the main tourist centres. If the mountainous terrain puts you off, join an organised tour where bikes and cyclists are transported up the mountain, enabling you to enjoy the scenic ride downhill.

Driving

Cretans like to boast about their dare-devil driving skills but in reality it is only the taxi drivers and a few flash drivers of expensive cars that behave badly on the roads of Crete. Most people stick to a sedate speed (forced to do so by the steep, twisting terrain) except on the main east–west National Highway, where locals often break the official speed limit (90kph/56mph) and overtake on bends.

The National Highway is the island's main artery, running east–west across the top of the island. It is a good wide road, but, despite appearances, it is not a dual carriageway. The right-hand lane is only used if you want to pull over to let a faster car past – it combines the functions of a crawler lane and hard shoulder. It is not a continuous carriageway, and disappears altogether from time to time. You may also find vehicles, flocks of sheep and roadside stalls blocking this lane.

The island's other roads all feed into the National Highway, running north, or – more often – south from it. These roads vary in quality from fast, wide, metalled roads with few bends to dirt tracks with massive potholes. However, many of the worst roads are currently being resurfaced. In general, roads running south are steep, twisting and slow-going.

During the rainy season (late October to early April), expect rock falls and

You'll find Zorbas at every turn – sure to attract custom

landslides to hamper your progress and be very wary of driving over rough roads – it is easy to damage the rim of your wheels and end up with a flat tyre. Where there is only room for one car to pass, the Cretans tend to be aggressive; it is wise to let Cretans go first, but do not flash your lights to indicate that you are giving way – on Crete, flashed lights mean 'get out of the way, I'm coming through!'

Practicalities

There are almost as many car rental agencies on Crete as there are restaurants and bars, so shop around for the best all-in deal – that is, one that includes comprehensive insurance, collision damage waiver and no mileage charges.

Drive on the right, wear seat belts in front and rear seats, and observe the speed limits: 50kph (31mph) in town, 70kph (43mph) on ordinary roads, and 90kph (56mph) for cars, 70kph (43mph) for other vehicles, on the National Highway. Drunken driving is severely penalised. Petrol stations are ubiquitous and open long hours. Road signs are in English and Greek except in out-of-the-way places.

Electricity

Standard two-pin continental-type plugs are used on Crete and the supply is 220 volts/50 cycles. Visitors from the UK and the USA/Canada need an adaptor.

Embassies

There is a British consulate at *Papalexándrou 16, Iraklíon (tel: (2810) 224012)*, but most other embassies are

Conversion Table		
FROM	TO	MULTIPLY BY
Inches	Centimetres	2.54
Feet	Metres	0.3048
Yards	Metres	0.9144
Miles	Kilometres	1.6090
Acres	Hectares	0.4047
Gallons	Litres	4.5460
Ounces	Grams	28.35
Pounds	Grams	453.6
Pounds	Kilograms	0.4536
Tons	Tonnes	1.0160

To convert back, for example from centimetres to inches, divide by the number in the third column.

Men's Suits

UK	36	38	40	42	44	46	48
Rest of Europe	46	48	50	52	54	56	58
USA	36	38	40	42	44	46	48

Dress Sizes

UK	8	10	12	14	16	18
France	36	38	40	42	44	46
Italy	38	40	42	44	46	48
Rest of Europe	34	36	38	40	42	44
USA	6	8	10	12	14	16

Men's Shirts

UK	14	14.5	15	15.5	16	16.5	17
Rest of Europe	36	37	38	39/40	41	42	43
USA	14	14.5	15	15.5	16	16.5	17

Men's Shoes

UK	7	7.5	8.5	9.5	10.5	11	
Rest of Europe	41	42	43	44	45	46	
USA	8	8.5	9.5	10.5	11.5	12	

Women's Shoes

UK	4.5	5	5.5	6	6.5	7	
Rest of Europe	38	38	39	39	40	41	
USA	6	6.5	7	7.5	8	8.5	

Fishing boat well equipped for the catch

in Athens. If you need help, go to the tourist police in the first instance (*see* Police, *p186*).

Emergency telephone numbers
Police *100*
Ambulance *166*
Road Assistance *104*

Health
The greatest hazards to health on Crete are the sun, sea creatures and mosquitoes. It is very easy to burn in the sun, even just walking around, and even in the relatively mild spring weather, especially if you are exploring archaeological sites on exposed hillsides – wear a hat to protect your head and neck, and cover your arms. Jellyfish can give you a nasty nettle-like sting that takes up to a week to go down. There is no cure but patience and time, though the ammonia in urine is said to have a mildly relieving effect. Sea urchin spines are a greater hazard – these black creatures inhabit rocky shorelines and are nearly invisible against the rock, so always wear shoes or sandals when exploring rock pools. Spines can be extracted, like splinters, using a needle, but seek medical help if they go deep – they can go septic if not removed.

The most effective mosquito deterrents are the plug-in electrical devices that are widely available on Crete. The green pyrethrum insect repellent coils (*spíres* in Greek) are also fairly effective, but by no means foolproof, so take insect-bite cream.

Basic emergency care is free and there are good health clinics providing outpatient services from 8am to noon in every large town. These are signposted (with a red cross) and are easy to find.

EU residents should obtain a European Health Insurance Card (available online at *www.ehic.org.uk*, from the post office or *tel: 0845 606 2030*) before travelling. As this does not cover all health costs and never covers repatriation costs, it is advisable to take out adequate travel insurance as well.

Language
Cretans are great Anglophiles, and they watch English and American television programmes, so almost everyone speaks basic English. Even so, the ability to read Greek characters will enrich your visit. Take care to get the stress right: every Greek word has an accent (´) over the stressed syllable, and if you get it wrong you are not likely to be understood (*see opposite*).

Lost property
Cretans are instinctively honest and helpful and will turn in anything they find that they recognise to be important or valuable. Go to the tourist police if all else fails.

It is helpful to know the Greek alphabet so that you can recognise place names, while the few words and phrases following the alphabet will also come in handy.

THE GREEK ALPHABET

Greek	Name	Pronounced	Greek	Name	Pronounced
A α	alpha	a	M μ	mi	m
B β	beta	b	N ν	ni	n
Γ γ	gamma	g, but becomes y in front of e and i	Ξ ξ	xi	x
			O o	omicron	o
			Π π	pi	p
			P ρ	rho	r
Δ δ	delta	d	Σ σ	sigma	s
E ε	epsilon	e as in extra	T τ	taf	t
Z ζ	zeta	z	Υ υ	ypsilon	u
H η	eta	e as in eat	Φ φ	phi	ph
Θ θ	theta	th	X χ	chi	ch as in loch
I ι	iota	i	Ψ ψ	psi	ps
K κ	kappa	k	Ω ω	omega	long o
Λ λ	lamda	l			

BASIC VOCABULARY

good morning	kaliméra
good evening	kalispéra
goodnight	kaliníkhta
hello	yásou
thank you	efkharistó
please/you're welcome	parakaló
yes	né
no	óchi
where is...?	pou iné?
how much is...?	póso káni?
do you speak English?	miláte angliká?
I don't speak Greek	dhen miló elinika

NUMBERS

1	éna
2	dhío
3	tria
4	téssera
5	pénde
6	éxi
7	evtá
8	okhtó
9	enéa
10	dhéka

PLACES

street	odós
square	plateía
avenue	leofóros
room	dhomátio
post office	tachidhromió
police	astinomía
pharmacy	farmakío
doctor	iatrós
bank	trápeza
café	kafeníon

FOOD AND DRINK

food	fagitó
bread	psomí
water	neró
wine	krasí
beer	bira
coffee	kafé
lobster	astakós
squid	kalamária
octopus	oktapódhi
red mullet	barboúnia
whitebait	marídhes
lamb	arnáki
chicken	kotópoulo
meat balls	keftédhes
skewered meat	souvlákia
pork	chirini
spinach	spanáki
courgette	kolokíthia
beans	fasoles
chips	patátes tiganítes
cucumber	angouri
tomato	tomáta
olives	elíes
salad with feta	horiatíki
tomato salad	saláta
yoghurt cucumber dip	tsatsíki

A bell tower silhouetted against the setting sun

Maps

The best general maps of Crete currently available are the *Nelles* and *Freytag & Berndt* maps and the *Bartholomew Crete Holiday Map*. For walking, it is best to use the excellent *Harms Verlag* 1:100,000 two-map set, which shows most of the footpaths. They are not widely available on Crete, so it is best to order them before you go from a specialist map shop.

Media

All your favourite newspapers (and many magazines) are sold on Crete, the day after publication. Cretan TV broadcasts many films and programmes in English (with Greek subtitles) and one channel is devoted to USA news.

Money and tax

The euro (€) is the unit of currency used in Crete. There are seven denominations of the euro note: €5, €10, €20, €50, €100, €200 and €500; eight denominations of coins: 1 cent, 2 cents, 5 cents, 10 cents, 20 cents, 50 cents, and €1 and €2.

Money-changers are ubiquitous, and some operate round the clock in big resorts. Commission rates vary enormously and it's worth shopping around to see who offers the best combination of exchange rate and commission. The worst rates are generally those of travel agents and hotels. Government tourist offices offer exchange facilities with rates that are similar to or lower than those of banks.

Major credit cards are accepted in main hotels, shops and restaurants, but not in cheap tavernas.

As in all EU countries, visitors from outside the EU can reclaim the Value Added Tax (VAT) (which can be as much as 20 per cent) on high-value purchases – ask about the Tax Free Shopping scheme.

If you need to transfer money quickly, you can use the MoneyGram[SM] Money Transfer service. For more details in the UK, telephone Freephone *0800 897198*.

The Thomas Cook website, at *www.thomascook.com*, provides up-to-the-minute details of Thomas Cook's travel services.

National holidays

Offices, banks and some shops close on national holidays, though in tourist resorts it is business as usual as long as there is money to be made. The dates of Lent, Easter and other religious holidays in the Orthodox calendar vary from year to year and can be up to two weeks later in the year than the equivalent feasts in the Western church calendar.

New Year's Day 1 January
Epiphany 6 January
Clean Monday Variable – two days before Ash Wednesday
Independence Day 25 March
Good Friday Variable
Easter Monday Variable
Labour Day 1 May
Ascension Day Variable
Whit Monday Variable
Assumption Day 15 August
Okhi ('No') Day 28 October
Christmas 25 December
St Stephen's Day 26 December

Opening hours
Museums and archaeological sites
Opening hours vary considerably and change with alarming frequency. Most museums and archaeological sites are open all day every day in summer, although a few close at 3pm and all day on Monday. Opening hours are shorter in winter.

Shops Stores catering to tourists open very long hours – typically from 10am to 10pm, or later. Street kiosks – selling everything from fruit and cold drinks to aspirins and razor blades – stay open even longer – some city kiosks never close. Shops and markets catering to the local population open 8am to 1.30pm Monday to Saturday, and 5.30pm to 8.30pm on Tuesday, Thursday and Friday only.

Monasteries and churches Most monasteries close in the afternoon for two or three hours, though the heavily visited ones remain open all day. If churches are locked, it is polite to respect the privacy of the keyholder during the siesta hours of 1–5pm.

Banks Typical hours are 8am–2pm, Monday–Thursday and 8am–1.30pm on Friday, but those in major resorts will open until later in the day.

Post offices Typical hours are 7.30am–2pm Monday–Friday.

Pharmacies
In Greek towns, the ØAPMAKAION (*Farmakeion*) serves the role of doctor and dispensary – the trained pharmacists who staff them can diagnose most common complaints and recommend a remedy. Though they observe the same opening times as local shops, there will always be one open on a late-night rota, details of which are posted on pharmacy doors or windows.

Places of worship
Orthodox churches are a prominent feature of every town and village – with luck you will be able to witness a wedding, or a naming ceremony (similar to christening); these usually take place on a Saturday and Sunday, respectively. There are no Protestant, Jewish or Islamic places of worship on Crete, but there are Roman Catholic churches in Iraklíon (on Odós Patros Antoniou) and in Chaniá (just south of the Archaeological Museum).

Police

Crete's tourist police are specifically trained to deal with common visitor problems and most speak English fluently. Many of the complaints they handle (such as cases of overcharging in restaurants and hotels) involve misunderstandings, rather than deliberate fraud, so they are principally there as diplomats to smooth ruffled feathers, but they will also swing into a sympathetic action if you are lost, stranded or just plain confused.

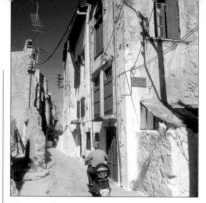

There are places on Crete where a car can't go

Dial 174 from anywhere and ask for information and help, or you can go to a specific tourist police station. The main ones are located in the following places:

Iraklíon *on Odós Dhikeosínis 10.*
Réthymno *on Prokimeá Venizélou* (i.e. on the beachside road) in the same building as the tourist information office.
Chaniá *on Odós Karaiskáki.*

Regular police are more unpredictable. Much of the time, they ignore activities that are strictly against the law (parking in prohibited areas, nude or topless bathing, camping rough, breaking the speed limit). Occasionally, however, someone orders a clampdown, so be wary and avoid drawing attention to yourself by behaving in a conspicuous or insensitive manner. Be polite if you are approached by a policeman and usually you will be let off with a warning.

Post

You can buy stamps from kiosks and shops, but they make a small surcharge which you can avoid by going to a yellow post office caravan – these are to be found on the main square of major towns and are open 7.30am–2pm (8pm in tourist areas) daily, with reduced hours on Sunday. In Iraklíon, the caravan is on the western side of Plateía Venizélou, by the entrance to the El Greco Park. In Chaniá it is on the cathedral square, off Odós Hálidhon.

Public transport

Crete is covered by a comprehensive bus network with hourly services on the busy routes between the four provincial capitals, and four or five services a day on routes covering other parts of the island. To the really remote villages, however, the service is restricted to one or two buses a day. Timetables are available at the tourist information offices and at the bus stations in the four main cities, all of which are centrally located. Tickets are purchased in advance from kiosks at the bus terminus, but are sold on board the bus if you join at a stop en route. Prices are very reasonable, and the buses are clean and comfortable.

Taxis

Taxis are used for long-distance journeys, as well as short trips across town. There are fixed fares for some journeys but you should always check and agree to the fare in advance to avoid misunderstanding. You can also hire taxis by the day or half day for sightseeing, and you can book taxis to drop you and return to collect you later in the day – for example, at the beginning and end of the Samaria Gorge walk.

Coaches

Signing up for one of the ubiquitous coach excursions offered by travel agents in every Cretan town is another way of getting to the most popular destinations – the main advantage being that the logistics are all handled for you.

Senior citizens

Most museums and archaeological sites have reduced rates for senior citizens. There are few other concessions, but, not being tied to school holidays, senior citizens can visit Crete at the quietest and cheapest times of the year. Room rates are lowest in April, May and October and, if you choose to overwinter in Crete, self-catering accommodation is remarkably cheap.

Student and youth travel

Holders of international student identity cards qualify for reduced-price admission to most museums. Crete is, in many respects, a cheap destination, and popular with young people as a result. Some come to Crete for the whole season, doing casual work in bars, tavernas or shops. The pay is poor, or nonexistent, but you may be given free accommodation, paid a commission, or allowed to keep the tips.

Sustainable tourism

Thomas Cook is a strong advocate of ethical and fairly traded tourism and believes that the travel experience should be as good for the places visited as it is for the people who visit them. That's why we firmly support The Travel Foundation, a charity that develops solutions to help improve and protect holiday destinations, their environment, traditions and culture. To find out what you can do to make a positive difference to the places you travel to and the people who live there, please visit *www.thetravelfoundation.org.uk*

Telephones

Card-operated pay-phones for local and international calls are everywhere in Crete – in shops, cafés, hotels and street booths. Coin-operated pay-phones are less common these days. You can also use the phone at the street-side kiosks; calls are metered and you pay at the end.

For long-distance calls it is cheapest to use a booth accepting phonecards, available from kiosks or shops, or to go to one of the OTE offices that are found in nearly every town (opening hours vary from round-the-clock in Iraklíon and Chaniá, to 6am–midnight in major resorts, to 7.30am to as early as 3pm elsewhere). Calls are metered.

For calls outside Greece, dial 00 + the country code + area code (minus the initial 0) + subscriber number:

Australia *61*	**UK** *44*
Eire *353*	**USA** and **Canada** *1*
New Zealand *64*	

For reverse charges dial the international operator on *161*. You may find it difficult to place an international call at peak times.

Time
Crete is two hours ahead of GMT all year round.

Tipping
Tips are expected on Crete (in some cases, this is the only source of income for the waiters and bar staff), so round up the figures to the nearest whole number or leave the small change in cafés and tavernas. Taxi drivers expect around 10 per cent, and a small tip should be placed in the toilet attendant's dish before using public facilities. It is also customary to tip tour guides and to give a small donation to priests if they open up the church for you and give you a tour.

Toilets
Public toilets are available in most towns, but often hidden somewhere easy to overlook, so most people use café toilets (which are much better) – having first ordered a drink. Toilet and shower blocks are found at most of the popular beaches, but their cleanliness varies. Remember, too, that toilet tissues should never be flushed down the toilet, but put into the wastepaper basket provided.

Tourist information
Branches of the official Greek National Tourist Organisations (EOT) can be found in the provincial capitals:
Iraklíon *Odós Xanthoudídou 1 (opposite the entrance to the Archaeology Museum).* The office seems always on the verge of being moved, but for the present remains here. *Tel: (2810) 228203/228225.*

Chaniá *Odós Khydonías 29 (inside Town Hall).*
Tel: (28210) 36155.
Réthymno *Prokiméa E Venizélou (the waterfront promenade).*
Tel: (28310) 29148.
Ágios Nikólaos *Aktí I Koundoúrou 20 (facing Voulisméni Lake).*
Tel: (28410) 22357.
Some useful websites include:
http://stigmes.gr/br/
www.creteisland.gr/
www.explorecrete.com/
www.interkriti.org
www.infocrete.com
http://cretetravel.com

Overseas offices of the Greek National Tourist Office are in:
UK *4 Conduit Street, London W1R ODJ.*
Tel: (020) 7495 4300.
USA *645 Fifth Avenue, Olympic Tower, New York, NY 10022.*
Tel: (212) 421 5777.
Also in Chicago and Los Angeles.
Australia *51–57 Pitt Street, Sydney, NSW 2000.*
Tel: (2) 9241 1663.
Canada *91 Scollard Street, 2nd floor, Toronto, Ontario M5R 1GR. Tel: (416) 968 2220.* Also in Montreal.

Travellers with disabilities
Tour operators will tell you which of their villas or hotels is best equipped for travellers who have special needs. A number of the major sights can be visited by booking on to excursions (Knossós included), but the steps and rocky terrain of many of the archaeological sites render them inaccessible to wheelchairs.

A
accommodation
  camping 178–9
  hotels 174
  rent rooms 174–5
  villas and
    self-catering 174
Agía Aikaterínis 38–9, 87
Agía Anna 141
Agía Foteiní 141
Agía Fotinis (church) 117
Agía Paraskeví 141
Agía Rouméli 128
Agía Triáda 46–7, 91, 100–01
Agía Varvára 91
Ágios Cyrgiánnis 136
Ágios Efíchios 140–41
Ágios Giórgios 64, 169
Ágios Giórgios (church) 47
Ágios Ioánnis 108
Ágios Konstantínos 89
Ágios Márcos 87
Ágios Nikólaos
  24, 25, 26, 42–3
  restaurants 168
  shopping 152–3
Ágios Stéphanos 111
Ágios Títos 48, 84, 87
agriculture 78–9, 176
airports 178
Akrotíri peninsula 100–01
Alíkampos 144
Alikanós 136
Almirós River 130, 161
Almrída 130–31, 163
Amári 141
Amári Valley 140–41
Anemóspili 41
Ano Zákros 80
Anópoli 106, 145, 151
Anógia 102, 156–7
Aposelémis river 88
Áptera 130
aquifers (underground
  reservoirs) 64
Arádena 107
Arádena Gorge 92, 107
Arádiana 145, 151
Arbitration of Magnesia 70
Archaeological Museum,
  Archánes 42
Archaeological Museum,
  Ágios Nikólaos 42
Archaeological Museum,
  Iraklíon 30–33
Archaeological Museum,
  Chaniá 96–7, 133
Archaeological Museum,
  Réthymno 123–5
Archaeological Museum,
  Sitía 74
Archánes 40–41, 168
Arménoi 142, 151
arts festivals 19
Ayíi Pántes 76

B
banks 185
basketry 79
beach holidays 21
beaches 163

eastern Crete 25
western Crete 92, 130–31
bike hire 180
boat trips see ferry services
Boxer Rhyton 32, 47
Bull's Head Rhyton 31
bus services 186–7
business and overseas
  investment 176, 177

C
camping 178–9
car rental 21, 180
caves
  Daskaloyiánnis,
    Cave of 106
  Díktaean Cave
    6, 26, 72–3, 89
  Ídaean Cave 6, 34, 92,
    102–3
  Mátala 68
  Trapéza (Krónio) Cave
    64, 89
Centre of Contemporary
  Art, Réthymno 134
Chaniá
  13, 92, 93, 96–9, 132–3
  airport 178
  Archaeological Museum
    96–7, 133
  Firkás 96, 99, 133
  Historical Museum 97–8
  Kastélli 96
  Mosque of the
    Janissaries 96
  Naval Museum 98–9
  Renieri Gate 133
  restaurants 170–71
  shopping 152, 154
  Turkish Baths 133
  walk 132–3
Chaniá (province) 13, 92
Chersónisou 25, 67, 162
Chestnut Villages 139
Chieftain Cup 32, 46
children on holiday 160–1, 179
Chóra Sfakíon
  21, 106, 128, 145, 148
churches and monasteries 23
  Agía Aikateríni 38–9, 87
  Agía Anna 141
  Agía Fotinis 117
  Agía Paraskeví 141
  Agía Triáda 100–01
  Ágios Cyrgiánnis 136
  Ágios Efíchios 140–41
  Ágios Giórgios 47
  Ágios Ioánnis 108
  Ágios Márcos 87
  Ágios Stéphanos 111
  Ágios Títos 48, 84, 87
  Byzantine 84–5
  dress code 22
  Episkopí 51
  frescoes 84–5
  Gouvernéto 101
  iconostasis 84
  Katholikó 101
  at Meskiá 137
  Mikhaíl Arkhángelos
    (Arádena) 107

Mikhaíl Archángelos
  (near Máleme) 111
Moní Arkadíou 114–15
Moní Asomáton 141
Moní Chryso-
  skalitisses 138
Moní Goniás 108–9
Moní Kápsa 51
Moní Kerá 88
Moní Préveli
  116–17, 142
Moní Tóplou 70–71
Moní Varsamónero
  82, 91
Moní Vrontísiou 82, 91
  opening hours 22, 185
Panagía, Alíkampos 144
Panagía, Fódele 103
Panagía, Méronas 141
Panagía Kerá 62–3
Panagía Vatiótissa 40
Profítis Ilías 100
  at Samonás 130
  at Spiliá 110
  at Thrónos 141
cinema 159
climate and seasons
  148, 150, 179
coach excursions 187
conference centre 177
conversion tables 179, 181
costume, traditional 16
crafts
  basketry 79
  pottery 79, 156
  weaving 79, 102, 156–7
Cretan Ethnology,
  Museum of 78–9, 91
crime 179
culture see people and
  culture
currency exchange 184
customs and etiquette 15
customs regulations 180
cyclamen 111, 150
cycling 180

D
Damaskinós, Mikhaíl 38, 82
dance, traditional 159
Daskaloyiánnis,
  Cave of 106
Díktaean Cave
  6, 26, 72–3, 89
Diktýnna 104, 108
Díkte mountains 72
disabilities,
  travellers with 188
discos 158
diving 163
Dríros 77
driving
  car rental 21, 181
  regulations 180–81
  road systems 180–81
duty-free allowances 179–80

E
Easter 18–19
eastern Crete 20, 24–89
economy 176–7

El Greco 36, 38, 83, 103
Elafonísi islands 138–9
electricity 181
Eléfterna 114–15
Élos 139
Eloúnta 25, 77, 169
Elyros 121
embassies 181–2
emergency telephone
  numbers 182
entertainment
  cinema 159
  Cretan music 159
  dancing 159
  discos 158
Epimenides 73
Episkopí 51
Evans, Arthur 10, 11, 44,
  52, 56, 60–61
exploring the island
  5, 20–21

F
Falásarna 105, 138
Farangi Ínvrou see
  Ínvros Gorge
Farangi Kourtaliótiko see
  Kourtaliótiko Ravine
Farangi Samariás see
  Samaria Gorge
Farangi Thérissiano see
  Thériso Gorge
ferry services
  106, 120–1, 160–61, 178
festivals
  arts festivals 19
  Easter 18–19
  saints' days 19
  wine and food 19, 74
Festós 26, 44–6, 90
Festós disc 31, 46
Fódele 102
Folk Museum, Ágios
  Konstantínos 89
Folk Museum, Ágios
  Giórgios 64
Folklore Museum, Sitía 74
food and drink
  alcohol 165
  for children 161
  coffee 165
  'comfort food' 164
  Cretan cuisine 164–5
  desserts 164–5
  grilled foods 164
  kafénion (café) 14
  menus 166
  restaurant prices 166
  restaurants 167–73
  tavernas 5, 164, 166
  traditional Cretan diet
    78, 164–5
  wine and food festivals
    19, 74
Fournés 136
Fourní 140–41
Fragkokástelo 107, 145

G
Gavalochóri 131
Gávdos 6, 121

geography of Crete 6–7
German War Cemetery 110, 151
Giorgióupoli 130, 172
Golden Stair 138
Goniés 88
Gortýs 48–9, 84, 91, 151
Gourniá 50
Gouvernéto 101
governance 12–13
Gulf of Iraklíon 88
Gulf of Kissamos 104
Gulf of Mirabello 76

H
Harvester Vase 32, 46
health advice 182
Historical Museum of Crete, Iraklíon 36–7
Historical Museum, Chaniá 97
history of Crete
    Battle of Crete 99, 112–13, 116–17
    chronology 8–9
    Minoan civilisation 4, 10–11
    Mycenaeans 11
    Turkish occupation 76–7, 116, 118, 126
    Venetian rule 124, 137
    War of Independence 100, 112–13, 114
    World War II 36–7, 99, 110, 112–13, 116–17
History and Folk Art Museum, Réthymno 135
Homer 11, 67, 75
hotels 174

I
ibex (krí-krí) 7, 76
icons 38–9
Ídaean Cave 6, 34, 92, 102–3
Ídhaiki Spilia see Ídaean Cave
Ierápetra 50–51, 169
Ímvros Gorge 92, 144–5, 149
Iraklíon 24, 26, 28–33, 36–9, 86–7
    airport 178
    Archaeological Museum 30–33
    Arsenal 30
    Ágios Márcos 87
    harbour 28–9
    Historical Museum of Crete 36–7
    Icon Museum 38–9
    Morosini Fountain 87
    ramparts 30
    restaurants 167–8
    shopping 152
    tomb of Nikos Kazantzákis 30
    Venetian fortress 28–9
    walk 86–7
Iraklíon (province) 13, 26
Iron Gates, Samariá Gorge 128
Ítanos 70

J
jellyfish 182

K
kafeníon (café) 14
Kalamáki 68
kalderími (footpaths) 146
Kallergi mountain refuge 149
Kalýves 128, 130
Kamáres 46
Kámpos 138
Kandanoleon, George 137
Karabé 121
Kastanochória 139
Kastélli (Kastélli Kissámou) 104, 139
Kastrí 121
Katholikó 101
Káto Karouzaná 67
Káto Zákros 80
Koutsomatádos 139
Katsenavas, Emmanuel 36
Kazantzákis Museum 68–9
Kazantzákis, Níkos 12, 30, 37, 68–9
Kazantzákis, Níkos, tomb of 30
Kefáli 139
Keramotí 138
Khortátzis, Yeóryios 141
Knossós 5, 22, 26, 52–9
Kólpos Iraklíou 88
Kolpos Kissámou 104
Kolpos Mesarás 47
Kolpos Mirampéllou 42
Kolymvári 108–9, 172–3
Kommós 68
Kotsifoú Gorge 143
Kourtaliotiko Ravine 92, 117, 142
Koutsourás 27
Krapis 144
Krási 88
Kritsá 62–3, 156

L
Lake Voulisméni 42–3
language 182, 183
Lassíthi Plain see Lassíthiou
Lassíthiou 13, 24, 26, 64, 88–9
Lató 64–5
Laws of Gortýs 49
Lefká Óri 76, 92, 106, 149
Lefkógia 143
Lissós 121
Litsárda 151
lost property 182
Loutró 106, 149
Lychnostatis Museum 67

M
Makritikos 52
Máleme 110, 112
Mália 25, 26, 66–7, 169
maps 184
    see also Contents

Margarítes 156
markets 15, 185
Mátala 21, 68, 91, 169
media 184
medical treatment 182
Megapótamos river 116, 117, 142
Méronas 141
Messará Bay 47
Mesklá 136–7
Mikhaíl Archángelos (Arádena) 107
Mikhaíl Archángelos (near Máleme) 111
Mílatos 67
Minoan civilisation 4, 10–11
Minoan sites
    Anemóspili 41
    Archánes 40, 168
    Arméni 142, 151
    Agía Triáda 46–7, 91
    Festós 26, 44–6, 91
    Gourniá 50
    Knossós 5, 22, 26, 52–9
    Kómmos 68
    Mália 25, 26, 66–7, 169
    The Nail 88
    Palecastro 71
    Tílisos 103
    Zákros 26, 60, 80–81
Mirabello Bay 76
Mitsotakis, Kostas 13
Mnimeio 136
Mokhós Plain 88
Monastiráki Gorge 51
money 184
Moní Arkadíou 114
Moní Asomáton 141
Moní Goniás 108–9
Moní Kapsá 51
Moní Kerá 88, 89
Moní Préveli 116–17, 142
Moní Toplóu 70–71
Moní Varsamónero 82, 91
Moní Vrontísiou 82, 91
mosquito deterrents 182
motorbike and scooter hire 21
Mount Psiloreítis/Ida see Tímios Stavrós
Mount Yioúktas 69
mountain ranges 6, 92, 149
museums and archaeological sites 22, 68, 160
    opening hours 22, 185
    photography 22
music, traditional 159
Mycenaeans 11
Myrthios 143
Myrtiá 68–9, 169
mythology 34–5
    Minotaur 34–5
    Theseus 34–5
    Zeus 6, 27, 34, 69, 72, 73, 102

N
The Nail 88
Napoleon 51

National Highway 180
national holidays 184–5
NATO military presence 13, 100
Naval Museum, Chaniá 98–9
Néo Chorió 130
Nerantziés Mosque 135
newspapers 184
nude bathing 163

O
opening hours
    banks 185
    monasteries and churches 185
    museums 185
    post offices 185
    shops 185
orange groves 93
Ormos Soúda 100, 101
Ormos Stómiou 138
Órosira Díkti 72

P
Páchnes 92, 149
Palecastro 71
Palecastro Kouros 75
Palaióchora 21, 120–21, 126, 163, 173
Palaiókapas 109
Palm Beach 25, 71, 143
Panagía, Alíkampos 144
Panagía, Fódele 103
Panagia, Méronas 141
Panagía Kerá 62
Panagía Vatiótissa 40
Páno Archánes 40
Parthenios 109
Pashley, Robert 70
Peak Sanctuary Rhyton 7, 32
people and culture
    crafts 79, 102, 156–7
    Cretan costume 16
    customs and etiquette 15
    dance 159
    festivals 18–19, 74
    icons 38–9
    music 159
    politics 12–13
    priests and monks 118–19
    rural life 14
    shepherds 17
pharmacies 185
photography 22
phrygana 7
places of worship 185
Plakiás 143
Plato 49, 102
plumbing 175, 188
police 186
Polirínia 104, 151
politics 12–13
post offices 186
pottery 79, 156
Praisós 75
Préveli 25
priests and monks 118–19
Profítis Ilías 100
provinces (nomoi) 13

Psarí Foráda 89
Psychró 72, 89, 170
Psiloreítis mountains 92, 102
public transport 186–7

R
rent rooms 174–5
Réthymno 15, 122–31
  Archaeological Museum
    123–5, 135
  Centre of Contemporary
    Art 134–5
  History and Folk Art
    Museum 125, 135
  Nerantziés Mosque 135
  restaurants 171–2
  Rimóndi Fountain 135
  shopping 152, 154–5
  Venetian fortress
    (Fortétza) 125–6
  Venetian harbour 134
  Venetian loggia 135
  walk 134–5
Réthymno (province) 13, 92
Rodopós peninsula 108
Roman Catholic
  churches 185–6
rural life 14

S
St Paul 73, 106
St Titus 48, 73, 87
saints' days 19
Samaria Gorge
  92, 126–8, 149
Samonás 130
Sanmicheli, Michele 30

sea urchins 182
self-catering
  accommodation 174
Selí Ambélou pass 89
Selia 151
senior citizens 187
shepherds 17
shopping 152–5
  opening hours 185
  Tax free
    shopping 184
Sidherespórtes 128
Sitia 51, 74–5, 170
  Archaeological
    museum 75
  Folklore Museum 74
Sívrita 141
Snake Goddess 10, 31, 50
Soúda Bay 100, 101
Soúda Bay Allied War
  Cemetery 101
Soúgia 121, 136
south coast 21, 27
Spiliá 110–11
Spinalónga island 76–7
Spinalónga peninsula 76
sport 162–3
Stavrós 100
Stómio Bay 138
student travel 187
Sultana Festival 74
sunburn 182
sustainable tourism 187

T
tavernas 5, 164, 166
taxis 186–7

telephones 187–8
television 184
Temple of Apollo
  Delphinios 77
Temple of Apollo Pythios 49
Temple of Asklepios 121
Temple of Isis & Serapis 49
Théra 11, 61
Thériso 137
Thériso Gorge 92, 136–7
Thrapsanó 156
Thrónos 141
Tílisos 103
time difference 188
Tímios Stavrós 92, 149
tipping 188
toilets 188
topless bathing 163
Topólia Gorge 139
touring holidays 20, 21, 175
tourism 176
tourist information 188
tourist police 186
Trapéza (Krónio) Cave 64, 89
Tripití Point 121
travelling to Crete 178
Tsouderós, Emmanuel 37
Turkish Baths, Chaniá 133
Tympáki 156
Tzermiádho 89, 168–9

V
Vái 25, 71
Value Added Tax 184
Vámos peninsula 19, 128,
  130–31, 151, 172–3
Varsamónero 82–3

Vasíliki 151
Vathýpetro 41
Venizélos, Eleftherias
  12, 68, 97, 100
Venizélos Graves 100
visas 178
voltage 181
Vóroi 78–9, 91
Voríza 91
Vrýses 130, 144

W
walking on Crete
  20–21, 146, 148
watersports 163
weaving 79, 102, 156–7
western Crete 20–21, 92–3
White Mountains see
  Lefka Óri
wildflowers 7, 102–3,
  111, 130–31, 149–51
wildlife 7, 76
windmills 64, 70, 89
windsurfing 163
Wooden Staircase 127
words and phrases 183

X
Xylóskalo 127

Y
Yerontoyiannis 51

Z
Zákros 26, 80–81
Zarós 82, 91

ACKNOWLEDGEMENTS
Thomas Cook Publishing wishes to thank the following photographers, libraries and associations for their assistance in the preparation of this book, to whom the copyright in the photographs belongs.
MARITIME MUSEUM OF CRETE 112
MARY EVANS PICTURE LIBRARY 34, 35
NATURE PHOTOGRAPHERS 111 (Bush Robin); 148 (Frank B Blackburn); 150, 151
NEIL SETCHFIELD 10, 12b, 31, 33, 52, 58, 59, 66, 92, 166
PICTURES COLOUR LIBRARY 43, 89, 96, 97, 105, 120, 122a, 132, 149, 153, 162a
SPECTRUM COLOUR LIBRARY 177
WORLD PICTURES 18b, 26, 30, 42, 44, 57, 73, 87, 93, 108, 110, 115, 131, 155, 159, 173

The remaining pictures are held in the AA PHOTO LIBRARY and were taken by: KEN PATERSON, with the exception of pages 6, 12a, 13, 16, 18a, 19, 22a, 23, 27, 28, 46, 48, 49, 53, 56, 60, 62, 65, 79, 85a, 91, 99, 101a, 101b, 102, 103, 104, 106, 107, 109, 118a, 124, 127, 146b, 154, 160, 174, 180, 182 which were taken by PHILIP ENTICKNAP, and pages 64, 135, 167 taken by WYN VOYSEY.

Index: MARIE LORIMER

Proofreading: JAN McCANN for CAMBRIDGE PUBLISHING MANAGEMENT LIMITED

Send your thoughts to
books@thomascook.com

We're committed to providing the very best up-to-date information in our travel guides and constantly strive to make them as useful as they can be. You can help us to improve future editions by letting us have your feedback. If you've made a wonderful discovery on your travels that we don't already feature, if you'd like to inform us about recent changes to anything that we do include, or if you simply want to let us know your thoughts about this guidebook and how we can make it even better – we'd love to hear from you.

Send us ideas, discoveries and recommendations today and then look out for your valuable input in the next edition of this title. And, as an extra 'thank you' from Thomas Cook Publishing, you'll be automatically entered into our exciting monthly prize draw.

Emails to the above address, or letters to Travellers Project Editor, Thomas Cook Publishing, PO Box 227, Unit 18, Coningsby Road, Peterborough PE3 8SB, UK.

Please don't forget to let us know which title your feedback refers to!